ENTREPRENEUR'S QUICK STAF

PROMPT
PUBLISH
PROFIT

A 3-STEP A.I. DRIVEN PROCESS ANYONE CAN USE TO GROW YOUR AUDIENCE, AUTHORITY & SALES

CARLA WHITE

FROM THE AUTHOR OF "IDEA TO IPHONE"

HIRO.FM PRESENTS: PROMPT, PUBLISH, PROFIT

A 3-Step A.I. Driven Process Anyone Can Use To Grow Your Audience, Authority and Profits

Copyright © 2023 by Hiro llc. All rights reserved. No part of this publication may be reproduced, distributed, or transmitted in any form or by any means, including photocopying, recording, or other electronic or mechanical methods, without the prior written permission of the publisher, except in the case of brief quotations embodied in critical reviews and certain other noncommercial uses permitted by copyright law.

For permission requests, speaking inquiries, and bulk order purchase options, email hello@hiro.fm.

www.hiro.fm

ISBN

Designed by Gratitude Labs

Printed in the United States of America

Publisher's Disclaimer

While the publisher and author have used their best efforts in preparing this book, they make no representations or warranties with respect to the accuracy of completeness of the contents of this book. The advice and strategies contained herein may not be suitable for your situation. You should consult with a profession where appropriate. Neither the publisher not the author shall be liable for any loss of profit or any other commercial damages, including but not limited to special, incidental, consequential or other damages.

The company, product and services names used in this book are for identification purposes only. All trademarks and registered trademarks are property of their perspective owners.

AI and new technologies are unleashing creativity in ways never possible before.

Some people will adopt and ride the tech wave to the top at breakneck speed, like riding a jet when they've been using a tricycle.

And others will just get left behind, eating the jet fuel and their own tears for breakfast."

- CARLA WHITE, FOUNDER AND CEO OF HIRO.FM

PROMPT - PUBLISH - PROFIT EXTRA

If you purchased this book on Amazon instead of though our website, you may not be receiving our **Prompt - Publish - Profit Extra**. We are constantly improving our prompt scripts and sending these out to the our readers. We know you're busy, so we want to make sure you have the quickest pointers to writing, marketing and making money. You can sign up for the pointers at: **promptpublishprofit.com/extra**

11 Ways This Guide Will Help You Become Famous

New technologies are changing the nature of every job at every company (starting yesterday) but **what most are missing is the currency of trust.**

Trust will be harder to get as we question what is real and what is fake. And without trust, your business will crumble.

The secret is to use future technologies to publish in record time and still gain massive amounts of trust so you can sell like crazy. How? By adding a human touch.

Research has shown that people form a deeper emotional connection with the content of an audiobook, compared to reading the same content in a physical book. This is because the human voice has the ability to convey emotion in a way that text on a page simply cannot.

It's no secret that podcasts are explosive for businesses because they can help you reach a wider audience, establish yourself as an expert in your field, and build massive trust with your customers.

Yet, what very few realize is how **audiobooks and private podcasts are blowing up what is already there.** Sprinkle in some automated text messages and a few notifications, and you're pouring fuel on the fire.

This intimate yet automated system will drop an atomic bomb on the industry, creating something that didn't exist before. And here's why...

1. You build this in a few hours, regardless of your tech skills

This system requires ZERO websites, membership sites, writing copy, making slides, or creating a single video. The tech is so simple that everything can be set up in a couple of hours to start attracting the right customers. This is faster and cheaper than posting on social media or running ads to an online challenge, workshop, webinar, or even a "quick Zoom call" (all outdated methods that can ruin your business if they don't convert into sales fast).

2. You instantly become an authority

High-quality audiobooks can quickly establish you as an expert in your field, rather than just a salesperson. It is important to be seen as an expert or advisor because If they are paying you for your advice, they need to know that what you say is valuable. The more effective you are at establishing yourself as an expert, the more successful you will be and the better clients you will attract.

3. You gain massive trust with far less effort

When people press play, it's like a party for their brain chemicals. Dopamine, oxytocin and serotonin surge as they work out, walk the dog or do chores - and listening to you makes them unconsciously feel connected to you on a deeper level.

That connection is called a parasocial relationship – more than just tuning in; they get to know YOU on an even deeper level.

4. Appointment settings become obsolete

You will be able to automate messages that replace your appointment setters. You can now have a system interacting with your customers 24/7/365. Consumers demand instant responses from businesses at all time, and you can offer it on autopilot.

5. Faster results for your audience means more repeat buyers

With undivided attention of audio, people get results faster. They don't lose focus – they listen intently and take action. As a result, their lives are completely revolutionized – all thanks to you for providing such an effortless solution.

6. Everything is one-tap instant

The future is instant access from your phone. Zoom calls, membership sites and tradition lead magnets don't hold the same weight as they did in 2019. With Hiro, you can set up your entire system so that it's both a personalized experience and effortless to the consumer as ordering dinner, watching a movie or getting a ride.

7. Fire your funnel builder (no hate, love you techies. It's just the inevitability of what's coming)

If you're struggling to keep up with the complexities of funnels, my system offers a breath of fresh air. Instead of battling through making funnels or marketing copy, you're about to discover and easier and faster way to capture an audience and turn them into paid clients — so that they can put your energy into areas of your business you love without sacrificing success.

8. Start with low risk and still get high returns

With this system, you can avoid that risk and still run your business like $10M industries. You can 100x your output with a fraction of the effort. And it doesn't require gambling on inventory, team members and systems. You don't have to go all in, ride or die.

9. You focus on your zone of genius while systems do the work

You can use artificial intelligence to create your outlines, content and promo copy. Do this in a day and have a full audiobook to promote your business. You can even have your AI voice read it. Think this is outlandish? I wrote this guide with AI.

10. You can finally stop depending on ads

With this system, you don't have to drive any traffic to your audio shows to make serious money. This tickles me pink, because that's a huge issue for many of you. Not all of you, but most of you are the achilles heel, the enemy of the profits that could be in your pocket.

11. You will stand out from the crowd so much that...

People will ask you how you did it. You're making twice the profits in half the work. But until then, if you're a first mover, this will make you stand out.

A Special Note for You

Hello Super Hiro!

You're about to discover...

- How to become an underground celebrity and reach millions of people using simple systems that you can get done in one day ... even if you're starting with zero audience right now

- How to build trust and create customers for life using one of entrepreneurs most underutilized tools at your disposal–your voice.

- How to scale sales to 7-figures and beyond using a proven roadmap that previously required an entire team to implement, but can now be done by one person.

But none of this will happen if you don't take action. In fact, you most likely will lose money and I don't want that to happen.

Fast action requires just three things:

1. **Go for done, not perfect** - This guide is designed to help you set up and launch quickly, not to create the perfect system. We can improve it later.

2. **Get an accountability partner** - Research shows that you will achieve better results if you work with a friend. Reach out to a few now and get them to build their own system with you.

3. **Get support & advice from others** - We created a free group on Facebook just for entrepreneurs like you. Our group is chuck full of brilliant, fun, and helpful people who are ready to support and encourage you on your entrepreneurial journey. Here's your link join: https://facebook.com/groups/superhiros

> **PRO TIP:** Version one is better than version none. Our goal is to get your book done!

Grab your free bonuses that we created to help you launch even faster.

Table of Contents

11 WAYS THIS GUIDE WILL HELP YOU BECOME FAMOUS	I
A SPECIAL NOTE FOR YOU	VII
ABOUT THIS QUICK START GUIDE	**13**
A Note About AI and Publishing	13
A Note About This Guide	14
WHO THIS GUIDE IS FOR	**17**
What Skeptics Are Saying	18
CHAPTER 1: HOW SOME CRAPPY MP3S MADE ME $103,000	**19**
CHAPTER 2: TRENDS EVERY BUSINESS NEEDS TO PAY ATTENTION TO RIGHT NOW	**33**
CHAPTER 3: YOUR AUTOMATED SELLING MACHINE™	**39**
Step 1: SMS opt-in to access your show (and grow your list)	40
Step 2: Leverage the power of audio without creating a podcast	41
Step 3: Automated messages to increase engagement	43
The process goes like this...	43
CHAPTER 4: PROMPT	**47**
From Writer's Block To Book In Record Time with ChatGPT	47
My Binge-Like-Netflix Formula™	48
Step 1: List The Top Problems You Solve	51
Step two: Match the problem to your solutions	52
The Perfect Audiobook Formula	53
AI Writing Tools	63

ix

CHAPTER 5: PUBLISH   69

How to free yourself from the system and publish your audiobook in minutes (not months)   69
Your Automated Selling Machine   69
The Cost Of Outdated Models   70
How To Get A Massive Subscriber List With One Word   74
The Fortune Is in the Follow Up — How to Seal the Deal with Just Three Text Messages   75
Creating Your Own Notifications   77
Message One: The Gift   78
Message Three: "Next steps"   79

CHAPTER 6: PROFIT   83

How to outsell the competition, even if they're industry giants   83
Ways To Profit   84
Buying Is Like Winning A Prize (Steal This Script)   84
A Single Social Media Post That Can Attract 100s of Listeners   87
What to do when people reply to your post   91
5 Effortless Audiobook Profits   92
An Absolute Must If You're On TV, Radio or Presenting From Stage   93
Go On A Virtual Book Tour   95
The $5 Ad Strategy   96

CHAPTER 7: THE FASTEST PATH TO AUDIO CASH   99

Ways To Profit From Existing Content   101
Case Studies   102
How To Create A Show Without Picking Up A Mic   104

CHAPTER 8: HOW TO GET FREE EXPOSURE TO THOUSANDS OF LISTENERS   107

CHAPTER 9: WHAT'S NEXT?   109

Introducing the Prompt Publish Profit Sprint   112

ABOUT THE AUTHOR	115
NEXT STEPS	117
WHAT OTHERS ARE SAYING ABOUT HIRO.FM	119
RESOURCES & CHECKLISTS	121
Software and Materials Needed:	121
Create Profile Checklist	121
Create Show Checklist	122
Setup Sales Page	123
Setup Keyword	124
Setup:	124
Test:	125
Automations Checklist	125
AI PROMPTS TO GET YOU STARTED	127
The Basics	127
Book Prompt Basics	129
Introduction	130

About This Quick Start Guide

A Note About AI and Publishing

So, you're probably wondering how the A.I. is going to fit into the world of publishing books and audiobooks. Well, buckle up, because it's about to get interesting.

See, marketers are going to try and use A.I. to create as much content as possible in order to flood the Internet. That means your prospects are going to be bombarded with 20 times more content than usual.

And you know what that means?
It's going to be harder than ever to get their attention.

But here's the good news: all those marketers who are going to spam the Internet with their A.I.-generated content? They're short-sited slackers.

And that's actually great news for you. Why?

Because the content they create is going to be lame and have zero personality. It might have bits of useful information, but that will just be filler.

Your prospects are going to see right through all this crap content and crave something with substance and personality.

So does that mean you should avoid using A.I.?

Absolutely not!

You can use it to create your first draft in an afternoon filled with interesting facts and stats. So all you have to do is polish it up, add some personality, and make it flow better.

When you take time to add in some pizazz, you'll immediately stand out as different and better. And you know what?

People love buying from someone who understands them, has character, is vulnerable and most of all, has personality, rather than just another slacker spouting filler. You're about to discover how to do that in a faction of the time while getting more attention and trust than ever before.

A Note About This Guide

You may be reading this because you're looking for a way to leverage new technologies to grow your profits. Not in a few months and after missing the wave. But today. Maybe you want extra cash for a dream car or pay off your house. Or you want to really go big and have an affluent lifestyle so you can move through the world with ease, knowing you have the power to get what you want.

I know exactly what it feels like to want consistent, predictable income. Just four years ago, I was living "product launch" to "product launch", working day and night to make ends meet, stuck in survival mode.

Yet, whenever I opened Instagram, I'd see people oozing success. Money and opportunities would simply gravitate to them like kids to candy. Smiling next to friends on a private jet headed somewhere important, or speaking on stages with thousands in the audience, or splashing in a pool with their kids, it was like they knew something that I clearly didn't.

I wanted to be like the ultra successful people sitting on that jet. I wanted a life where I could fly off for a week whenever I felt like it.

But I was drowning in a sea of web pages to build, emails to write, social media posts to create, videos to record and PDF's to edit-all before getting my kids up for school.

It turns out that these "tried and true" tactics (that I thought were the answer to my prayers) weren't just complicated and expensive but as outdated as the phone book. We live in an era where watching a movie and getting dinner or a ride to the airport is one-tap instant. We can write an entire book in a day and make art like Picasso in seconds. My business was moving forward on a tricycle.

I was down to our last $643.28 and I devoured every blog post, PDF, video and course to figure out how to survive. My lifesaver ended up being a makeshift "private podcasts". It wasn't even that good and it saved my business.

That janky private podcast was like my very best sales person working 24x7 doing all the heavy lifting for me so by time customers got on a call with me they were already sold. Why? It works perfectly in today's world.

I built a blueprint to creating your own "automated sales machine" regardless of your tech skills or business size. I outlined it for you in this guide along with stories from my life so you can see how hyper-automation completely changed the course of my career. And I also sprinkled in the frameworks and tools I used to bring it all together for myself and thousands of others just like you.

This guide will show you how to tap into the golden age of artificial intelligence, audio and automations to achieve greater financial growth for you and your family. **Creating content using AI is one thing, but having it make money for you on autopilot? Now that's next level stuff, my friend.**

As a former agency owner who woke up every morning worried about how I would get ahead, I know that it can all be turned around if you follow the steps that I'm going to lay out in the chapters ahead.

Before I created Hiro.fm (I'll share the story about that in the next chapter), I was named a Top Woman in Tech by Forbes, and before that, I was the first woman ever to create an iPhone app. This was back in 2007, when everybody laughed at me saying that apps were fad because their Blackberry would never be replaced. Today that app, called Gratitude Journal, is one of Apple's longest-running apps with over a decade-long track record in the top of the charts.

That led to being invited on *Oprah*, getting featured on NPR, BBC and in the *New York Times*, *USA Today*, *Entrepreneur* magazine, and countless other major publications across the globe. Apps became my thing, and I eventually published *Idea to iPhone* and started my own app agency.

I have the gift of spotting powerful opportunities when I see one. I can also explain complicated stuff so that a kid can understand.

Just like apps, AI, audio and automations aren't a passing fad. This is revolutionary.

Ready to change the world?

Who This Guide Is For

This guide is specifically designed for entrepreneurs—especially coaches, consultant, authors, event hosts or experts of any kind.

This guide is for

- Course creators
- Agency owners
- Coaches
- Consultants
- Event hosts
- Authors
- Experts
- Entrepreneurs of any kind...

Who want to

- Bring in highly-qualified and cashed-up customers who are ready to buy
- Share their best secrets without fear of piracy
- Sell their audiobooks without losing a large percentage to Audible
- Get paid the rates they deserve
- And have it all on autopilot so you can do more of what you love

What Skeptics Are Saying

Some say that creating an audiobook with AI and launching it in a weekend is unrealistic or that the quality of the audiobook will be poor because it was not carefully edited and produced. They may also argue that using AI to create an audiobook goes against the traditional methods of publishing and that it could be seen as dishonest or inauthentic.

But you're going to discover what is possible, regardless of your technical skills. This step-by-step guide can help you reach your financial goals in a fraction of time and effort. Forget the unproductive strategies - we'll show you which ones are proven and effective and modern.

This short book will give you the story behind the software, outline a proven system for profiting from publishing, and map out three super simple steps to get you up and running in as little as an afternoon.

Ready? Let's go!

CHAPTER 1: How Some Crappy MP3s Made Me $103,000

It was a random Tuesday morning in 2019 when I got the call. I thought it might be a student wanting a refund for a course he purchased years ago. Or the usual "Hi, I want to make the next Instagram app, but better. Oh, and my budget is $2.13." But before I could start reeling off stuff about making apps, the woman on the other end of the receiver introduced herself. Her name is Lydia. She is a high end designer in Monaco looking for a business coach and wanted to hire me. To say this was unexpected is an understatement. I have never made a sale so easily before.

"Uh, ok, that's great!" I said. *"What are you looking for, and what's your budget?"*

"$20,000 but if it costs more, that's fine."

The hair raised on the back of my neck. My jaw didn't just hit the floor—it floated down in a cloud of sparkles. Twenty thousand dollars without a single word from my well rehearsed sales script, defending my prices or offering a payment plan so low that it matched where my business was heading-rock bottom.

Then I asked her another brilliant question.

"Why me?"

She replied "I just binge listened to your challenge and I kept feeling this energetic connection. Like karmic soul mates."

Wait, what? She was hiring me because of "a magical connection" she felt simply by listening to my voice?

So instead of saying "I'd love to help you but I've never coached someone whose clients are Oligarchs, Sheiks and Formula One Drivers." I responded with "Oh yeah! I can be your business coach because I was born to do!"

Then I hung up the phone and started to panic.

Reality was that I usually attracted clients who wanted $100,000 services in exchange for "exposure", or lopsided partnerships where I did all the work, or a promise of their profits. It was exhausting.

I'd wake up every day and think "Oh, good morning unrealistic deadlines. How are you today? What's up "never-ending project"? Hanging in there, buddy?'"

Then I'd go about my day working on the same strategies that attracted the same clients all over again. This isn't what I wanted.

My constant worry was about money. It consumed me. I knew I'd never get out of the cycle if I kept taking on clients like this. I was sick of waking up and going to bed worrying about money. The worry felt like a throbbing headache that would never go away.

But the problem is that I built my business for a time when people read emails and watched videos longer than 17 seconds. Worse, all my tactics were also just like every other entrepreneur on the planet. It was predictable, tedious and hard.

Then suddenly an incredible businesswoman in Monaco, the capital of success, wanted to hire me because of a janky private podcast I threw together?

This was my chance to "Marie Kondo" my business and replace everything holding me back with simple private podcasts so that my customer's entire experience would be as effortless as calling an Uber or binge watching Netflix.

First to go was my live challenge. Challenges are week-long training events that usually take place online in a Facebook group and on Zoom. These challenges are a ton of work. When I first heard about challenges in my marketing circles, I was told that it was simple: "just open up Zoom and customers will jump in. You go through your training for a few days and then at the end, you pitch your offer and make a bunch of money".

The first thing I discovered is that I'm fighting for their attention against 37 other tabs open on their computer. They're on email, Facebook, Amazon, and Messenger and probably their phone too. They're catching a fraction of what I'm saying.

The next thing I discovered is anyone watching the reply felt more like they were just catching a random video from YouTube rather than a live event.

And last, which most don't talk about, is the dropout rate. I did everything to keep them engaged and get them to finish. But even the number one Netflix series can't keep a person coming back every day for a week.

And my problem was – if they didn't finish the challenge, they didn't hear my invitation to join my coaching program and they didn't buy.

I'm up at 4 a.m. and working on this, doing whatever I can to get people to show up. I'm posting on Facebook, sending them emails and texts, and I'm back at my computer again after kissing my boys goodnight because I have to post replays.

Instead of hanging out with my two little boys – I'm a mother of just the most adorable kids on the planet – who were the reason I was doing all of this. Instead of playing with them, I was at my computer at the crack of dawn, with all this complicated work, just to get people through the challenge.

After running the challenge over and over for a few months, I started to look at the numbers. If you ever hosted a challenge yourself, you might be familiar with these numbers:

TYPICAL CHALLENGE STATS

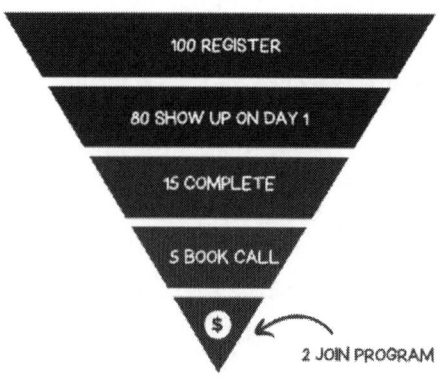

My typical stats for challenges

These are the numbers I had to work on to scale and I wasn't even close to hitting my goals. But the worst thing was that I felt I was letting my family down. I made them promises.

I remember, I'm sure this was one of the lowest parts of my career, when I was sitting at a table. My kids were there, my husband's there, and I'm there–physically, but not mentally.

My mind was working on some math. I had to calculate the hours between bedtime and getting the kids to school and whether it's enough to finish emails, video editing and two social media posts and some sleep. And my husband looks me flat in the eye. And he says, "It's about ten."

"Thank you!" I replied to a very confused face.

"It's about time...to stop all of this." he said waving his hands towards my laptop.

"Oh! About time!" To my defense, he does have a strong British accent. But he was right, I was a shell of myself.

I invested so much money and time into these launches that I tried every trick out there. I downloaded PDF's, watched videos, listened to countless books. And I was at a new low. Because I had success before and I didn't have to work until my eyes bled for it. I knew it was possible. But more so, I wanted more for our boys. I wanted to raise them how we planned to raise a family.

Then one day, a single email changed everything. A woman who joined my challenge realized that she can't make the lives, won't watch the replays, so I'm bracing myself for her refund request. Instead, she was wondering if I'd pull the audio from the videos so she could listen to challenge instead.

Now at this point in my career, I would do anything it took for them to succeed. If they wanted me to do a backflip, I'll do a backflip. Audios? No problem.

I uploaded 26 videos one by one to a website that allowed me to download the audio versions. Then, I placed all of the audio files in a Google Drive and sent the link to my client. A few days later, I was eating lunch and reading Facebook when I received a notification about a live video in our private group. I opened it to watch and what happened next changed my life forever.

The woman said: "*I downloaded everything in one day. So I come home and I'm like, I deserve to be wealthy. And I'm just really excited. And I was at my best. I was just a different person. And then a few days later, my son shared suicidal thoughts with me. We're in crisis. But I don't think he would have shared with me if I hadn't gone through this challenge.*"

One second I'm smashing the hearts and likes and the next I'm an emotional mess. I drop my sandwich, run to my computer and create my first private podcast to share with everyone who joined my challenge. I had no idea that this would lead to Lydia from Monaco hiring me, or dozens other just like her.

After moving from video to audio, nearly everyone in the challenge was able to complete it, and they even asked for more. They invited friends and family to my challenge, exploding my to word-of-mouth marketing, which is the best kind of marketing anyone could ask for.

An important note: my "private podcast" I gave them, which achieved a 70% completion rate, was far from perfect.

Yet I still got messages like this one:

> I listened to your talks on a five hour drive and they're absolutely off the charts. I'm going to be implementing these lessons immediately. You are so gifted my friend.

JOHN WARNER

Just one of the many messages I get from my audio products.

After saying goodbye to old ways and using a private podcast instead, I celebrated my first $100,000 month, paid-in-full, no financing or payment plans. Paid in full! I'll share how I did that in a minute. But first, I need to share *what* I had to do to achieve this not just once, but multiple times over time.

Running my challenge as a private podcast created a new problem: each time I ran the challenge, I had to spend a week recreating a 26-episode podcast. There wasn't a software on the planet that could automatically release episodes, expire access to the show, and keep my show privacy proof.

So, when the world shut down in 2020, I pulled out my software development tools, used what I learned while working at NASA, Microsoft, and Apple, and created Hiro.fm.

In August 2020, Hiro officially launched.

Right away, I had people messaging me wanting advice on how to add audio to their own businesses. I'd hop on calls, and in some cases, as with ClickFunnels founder Russell Brunson, guided them through the process.

Another person I talked to was Kiana Danial. I don't know if you've ever heard of her, but she's a *New York Times* bestseller and investment coach for women, especially moms.

At the time, she was trying to hit million in sales with her business but struggled with refund requests because her customers are happen to be the busiest people on the planet. They wanted to learn from Kiana but finding time was nearly impossible.

She reached out to learn how I was using private podcasts and we talked about using Hiro in her program. She decided to add audio to her business by turning her trainings into private podcasts. Not long after we started working together, she made over a million dollars in sales. Two years later, her sales have skyrocketed to over $10 million!

I was like, "huh, there must be something to this". Imagine the impact I could have if I took this informally approach and turned it into a system. What if I took the essence of what I was doing and put it into a step-by-step training program to really leverage the benefits of Hiro?

That's exactly what I did in October 2021. We called it Six Figure Hiro and each person who joined (I call them Super Hiro) paid me at least $2,000 to be a part of the training.

I broke down the exact process you're learning about today. We went through everything in great detail, from start to finish, on how to quickly set up a profitable private podcast from scratch using automations, audio, and artificial intelligence.

> **NOTE:** My 3-step system in this book has been updated to include new features in Hiro as well as emerging technologies like ARTIFICIAL INTELLIGENCE.

Some of those Super Hiros, like Nina Rocco, immediately saw results. This was a $6,000 result on something she'd never done before. She had a bricks and mortar business before. She never sold services online. She's a fitness coach, and it worked for her.

Then there's Raphy, an amazing guy who's a marriage coach. He told me, "Carla, I used your technique at a live event and we closed better than ever before".

To be clear, before working with me, Raphy had zero sales because he was brand new to online selling. After we added audio to his offers, he had a 17% conversion rate. You might not think that's a big deal, but I want to emphasize that he did this on his first try.

Have you been trying to make money online for more than six months? Or maybe even a year or longer without success? How much better it would be if your first attempt was profitable?

Before using the system I sharing with you today, I would have to hire a team of experts and gamble the family farm to make a sliver of a profit. Now, I give prospects my audiobook and calls are more like an onboarding calls and it only takes two hours to set up.

AUDIO SALES MACHINE INSTANT SAVINGS

Ad budget $0

Funnel budget $0

Copywriter budget $0

Tech pro budgets $0

Video budgets $0

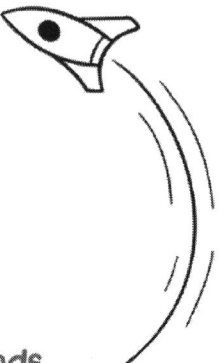

Time creating sites: 0 seconds

Time writing emails: 0 seconds

Time creating videos: 0 seconds

Time spent creating slides: 0 seconds

Just to give you some perspective, if you can get just twelve people to get your audiobook each week, around nine or ten of them will actually listen. You send those twelve people an automated message inviting them onto a call with you. Based on the industry-average close rate of 20%, this means that if you are selling a product or service for $3,000, you have the potential to earn almost $303,000 per year in net income.

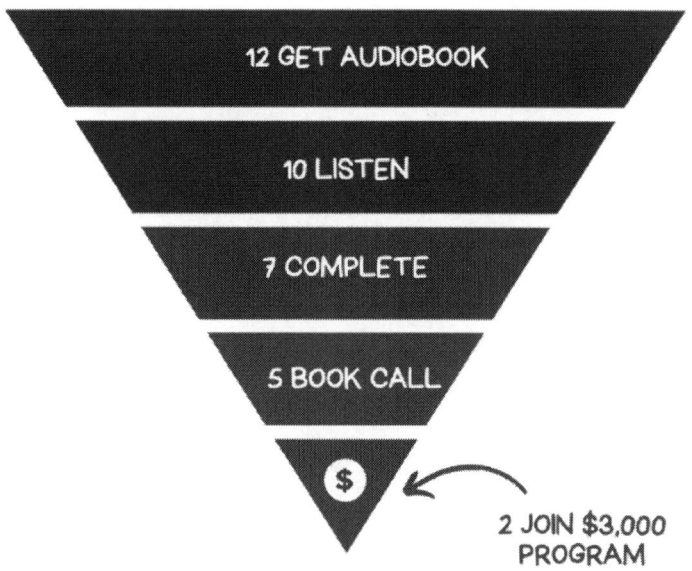

THE $312K A YEAR FORMULA
With just 12 people getting your book a week

If you have a coaching or consulting program higher than $3,000 per sale, congratulations! Your profit is far more than $303K. Now, this isn't the gross. This is what you take home. It's what you keep that matters. This is what's in your pocket, net profit, spendable "Money in Your Pocket" showing up in your bank account, after everything else is accounted for. This is an automatic income stream.

But let's say you just get one person to listen to your show a week. That is still $3,000 a month, which for many people can be the difference between sleeping at night or not. It's a house payment: it's a new car.

It's just you creating an audiobook or private podcast, getting one person to listen to it, and then sending a text or an email invite for them to jump onto a call with you (I break down the whole system in this guide). That's it. You could potentially make about $3,000 profit every month.

When you factor in the true cost of this model, both time and money, you won't find a more cost-effective, quick-to-setup, more impactful approach to financial growth.

For some, this is your shot at competing with the industry giants for a fraction of the costs. Imagine using ads to get 10,000 people to grab your audiobook. If you have just $1,000 worth of product, there is potential for over $1 million in profit - without lifting a finger!

I don't know if this excites you as much as me. But this is a game changer for those who are far superior with their services and need to get more attention.

I was on a mission to get this system out there and reach as many people as possible, but the thought of writing a book was intimidating. The process of writing can be challenging and emotionally taxing, and I had experienced my fair share of stress and anxiety from previous writing projects. However, I was determined to push past my fears and write this book, no matter how difficult it may be.

I even spent thousands of dollars hiring a professional to help me write it, but the work was rushed, quality was disappointing and the delivery was weeks past the deadline. Talk about a major waste of money!

I was stuck, and the words just weren't flowing. I was ready to throw in the towel and give up on my dream of getting this powerful book into the right hands.

But then, something miraculous happened. I finished my book in a day all while watching Argentina beat The Netherlands in the World Cup. How? With the help of artificial intelligence. And let me tell you, it was a game changer.

Using AI writing tools like ChatGPT, I was able to churn out my book in record time. The software helped me generate ideas, organize my thoughts, and even come up with killer headlines.

But it's not all about the technology. To really succeed at writing a book using AI, you need to have a solid understanding of how the process works and a proven strategy to profit from your work. And that's where this guide come in.

Next, I'm going to pull back the curtain and reveal the hyper-system that so few know about and will make you stand out head and shoulders from the competition.

The first step is to create your Hiro.fm account. So go to Hiro.fm and create your account if you don't have one. It's absolutely free.

Key Points:

- Businesses today are facing a rapidly changing world, yet many are still using marketing tactics from an era long gone. It's no secret that the traditional system is outdated, complicated, and often expensive.

- You might have heard about people making six or seven figure launches, but what they don't tell you is that they often spent just as much in expenses to get there.

- If you don't have a one-tap solution to build your authority, you are losing out. In the post-pandemic world, consumers want flexibility and convenience. They don't want to be tied down to web calls or stuck at a desk.

- With our process, you can reach them wherever they are and whenever they have time. And you don't need to gamble your entire savings to make it happen.

ACTION STEPS

1. Create your free Hiro trial (https://app.hiro.fm)
2. Set up your profile and connect your Stripe account following this guide: https://hiro.fm/quickstart
3. If you get stuck, reach out to our team (https://help.hiro.fm)
4. Congrats! You're already part way there!

Up Next:

The average American business spend $2.1 million per year just to get people's attention. People's attention span is now shorter than that of a goldfish and businesses are viciously competing for those fleeting moments of attention. But what if I told you that you don't have to spend millions of dollars in marketing to get people's attention? What if there's an easier way.

CHAPTER 2: Trends Every Business Needs To Pay Attention To Right Now

We all know that AI has taken over all the conversations. But we uncovered a second equally powerful trend that almost no one knows about and entrepreneurs have been using to make a fortune and that is audio.

Did you know that right now is the very best time to profit from audio better than any other time in history?

Here is a big reason why. **Attention is the new currency.**

Put simply, billionaires grow their wealth by controlling the world's scariest resources. In the past decades it was oil. Today they're doing it by controlling the world's scarcest resource - attention. Attention spans are shortening and competition is increasing, making it harder than ever to get it.

Here are three ways audio is disrupting that game.

HOW TO OUTSELL THE COMPETITION EVEN IF THEY'RE INDUSTRY GIANTS

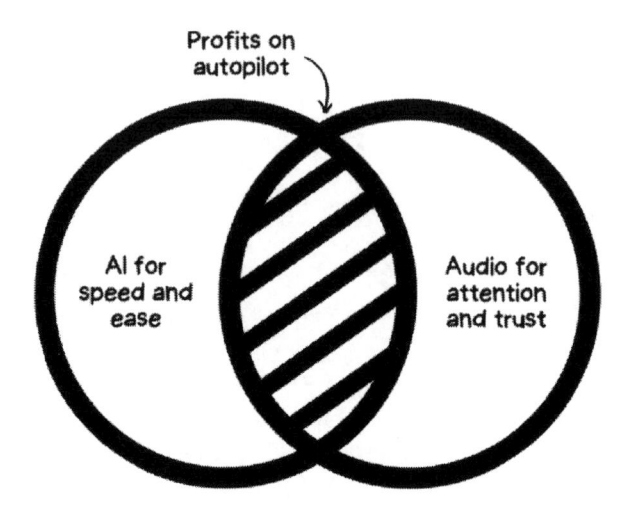

Profits on autopilot ↘

- AI for speed and ease
- Audio for attention and trust

1. Audio gets you more attention.

On average, short form videos get 7 seconds of attention. With ads, it's about 5 seconds before the viewer wanes and moves on. As a result, 97% of all programs fail or quit.

But audio is the great equalizer. With audio, you can break through the noise and reach far larger audiences than all your emails, videos, and posts combined. It's like a superpower - allowing your unique message to be spread further and faster than any other form of communication.

Research has shown that 80% of all audio content listeners consume all or most of the show. And they're listening on average to one hour and 29 minutes of audio content a day.

If you do the math, you are getting 314 times more attention than all those other resources, social media ads and emails combined!

Audio works where you're today, not just where I know you can be in the future. But you can do audio today to make money next week and next month.

HOW MUCH ATTENTION ARE YOU REALLY GETTING?

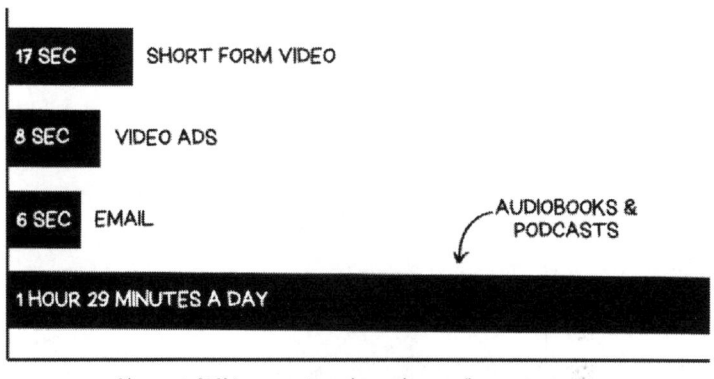

17 SEC	SHORT FORM VIDEO
8 SEC	VIDEO ADS
6 SEC	EMAIL
1 HOUR 29 MINUTES A DAY	AUDIOBOOKS & PODCASTS

You get 214X more attention using audio content

2. Audio listeners will spend more money.

It's also because of who is listening. Audio caters to twenty percent of the market that represent eighty percent of the buying power in every single market. This is a mathematical fact; this is the 80-20 rule. If you've heard of that, the law of the vital few, whatever you want to call it.

In the U.S., more Americans listen to audio content daily, then have Netflix accounts. And they have an average household income of $250,000. They have money!

This is where we want to fish. This is where the most money is being spent. This is where we want to dig for gold because this is where the gold will be found.

These people are hungry for knowledge and enthusiastic about finding the best solutions possible.

They are eager to dive in and discover more from you.

TYPICAL AUDIO LISTENER

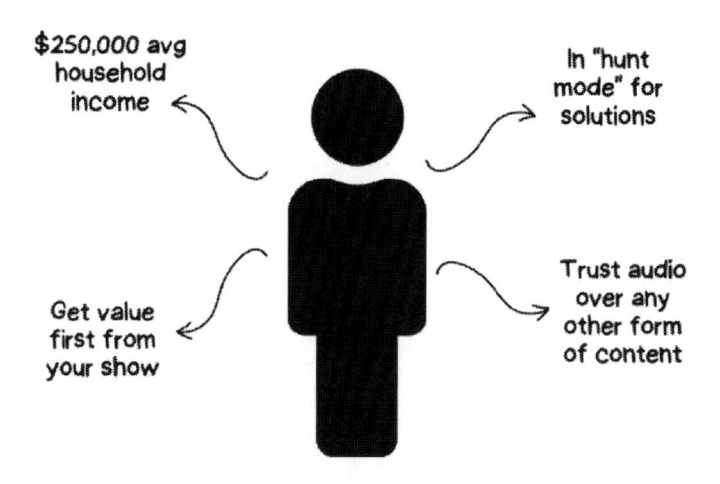

- $250,000 avg household income
- In "hunt mode" for solutions
- Get value first from your show
- Trust audio over any other form of content

As a show host, you have the opportunity to really connect with your listeners and give them something valuable. And they won't mind if you occasionally offer them something to purchase. If results come first, then it won't feel like a sales pitch when you invite listeners into a solution they need. That's why the audio revolution is in full swing and not turning down the volume soon!

Twitter, Facebook, Spotify, Amazon and YouTube have all invested heavily into the audio market. Even TikTok is getting into audio.

3. It's an untapped and rapidly growing market.

What most people don't seem to be aware of is the amount of people that are spending money on audio content. It's gone up 148 times since the first time I started this business. A thriving business that has made me hundreds of $1,000s when the market was 148 times smaller than it was today and twice as competitive.

Portable eLearning is at a record high - and it's not slowing down. In fact, with an estimated $645 billion industry by 2030 and more than a billion dollars are spent daily!

If you don't act now, you'll miss out on this golden era of audio. And it's not confusing; it's not complicated. If you ever listened to a podcast or audiobook, you already understand most of how it works.

The problem is people think "podcast" and believe it's time consuming and exhausting. What they don't seem to realize is that there is way to leverage to power of podcasts without all of that work. In fact, with the right strategies and techniques, you can leverage the power of audio to reach a wide audience and make a profit without spending all your time and energy on it.

Key Points:

- Audio lets you outsell the competition, even if they're industry giants.

- Audio is a powerful tool that works wherever you are right now, no matter your budget or marketing experience.

- Audio-learning is a multi-billion dollar industry that has a lot of untapped potential, giving you the chance to stand out and make a big impact.

- Audiobook sales are increasing while physical books are decreasing. This is a trend that will continue over the next decade.

- Audiobooks are faster, cheaper and easier to produce than short-form video, podcasts, emails, webinars and online trainings.

- Studies show that people trust audio content over any other form of content including written or video.

Up Next:

> Discover the system that can take you from zero to $250,000 without complicated funnels, expensive ads, or a massive email list. And the best part is that you'll be entering an industry that's worth billions of dollars and still has plenty of untapped potential. That means you'll have the opportunity to stand out in a crowded market and truly make a name for yourself.

Chapter 3: Your Automated Selling Machine™

This is my system made A-B-C simple and what we will set up for you by time you're done with this short guide. I'm going to break down my system in a way that's easy to understand and follow. We'll walk you through each step, making it simple and straightforward to implement. By the time you're done, you'll have everything you need to get your business up and running, without the need for complicated funnels, ads, or a big email list.

YOUR AUTOMATED SELLING MACHINE
People text to opt-in to your show, listen and become customers

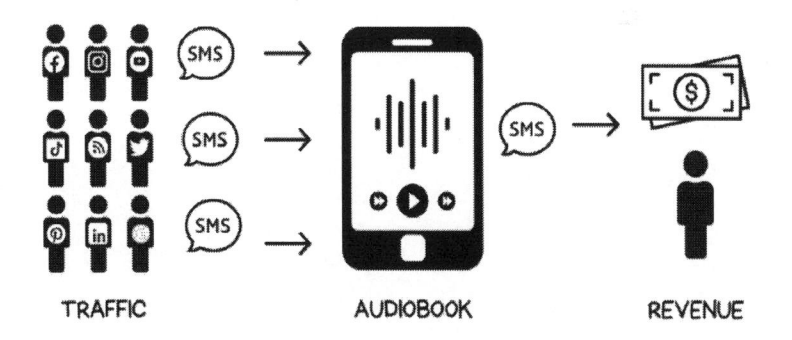

TRAFFIC — AUDIOBOOK — REVENUE

First, you go from unknown to famous pretty quickly. Before you go dismissing fame as insignificant, let me tell you that those famous folk are constantly doubling down on their fame game because they know just how darn lucrative it is. So don't knock it 'til you try it, baby. You want fame. So the first piece on the system lets you reach as many people as possible.

THE UNICORN

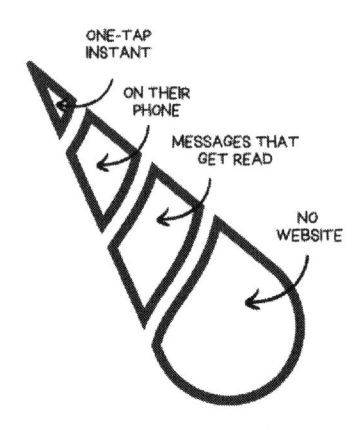

- ONE-TAP INSTANT
- ON THEIR PHONE
- MESSAGES THAT GET READ
- NO WEBSITE

The best thing about this model is that it's a frictionless funnel for your audience. A funnel is a marketing term that helps you visualize the process of someone's journey with you. Imagine a bunch of people coming into your world at the top of the funnel, and a few buyers coming out at the end. The more prospects come in, the more buyers come out. So our first goal is to get as many people to come in and the best way to do that is to make it easy for consumers.

Here's how it works.

Step 1: SMS opt-in to access your show (and grow your list)

People can get private access to your audiobook by texting one word to a personal phone number that Hiro gives to you. This single piece of the trail makes you famous by growing your subscriber list insanely fast. They text a word and in exchange you get their names, email addresses and phone numbers. This is pure gold.

Did you know that people open and read text messages almost immediately after receiving them? In fact, almost all text messages (99%) are opened within 10 seconds of being received. That's a lot better than emails which have a 17% chance of being opened. This one small change can make a big difference in your business.

You'll get a whole bunch of phone numbers you can use in marketing. In exchange for handing over a phone number and opting in with a keyword, your audience get access to your audiobook, which is the second piece of the trail.

EASIEST LIST BUILDER ON THE PLANET

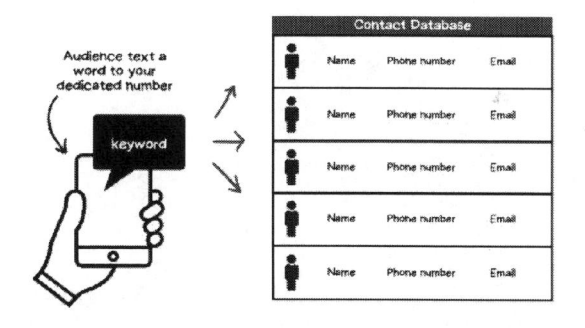

Step 2: Leverage the power of audio without creating a podcast

The future of the education is "on-the-go-learning". People don't sit down and intensely study a single skill at a time like they used to and long form courses don't hold the same weight as they did in 2019.

Instead, consumers who are serious about a solution find topic in their area of interest on iTunes, Spotify or Audible and listen as they're going about their day. They're also building a relationship with the creators.

What does this mean for you as a business owner? You have to deliver your expertise the same way. You have to get on their phones so they just have to pop in an earbud to learn.

Your audiobook is an easy way for people to go deeper with you. And once you've bonded, and built trust and credibility, they might come work with you. But only after you've proven you are an expert and can help them.

CUSTOMER LIFE CYCLE

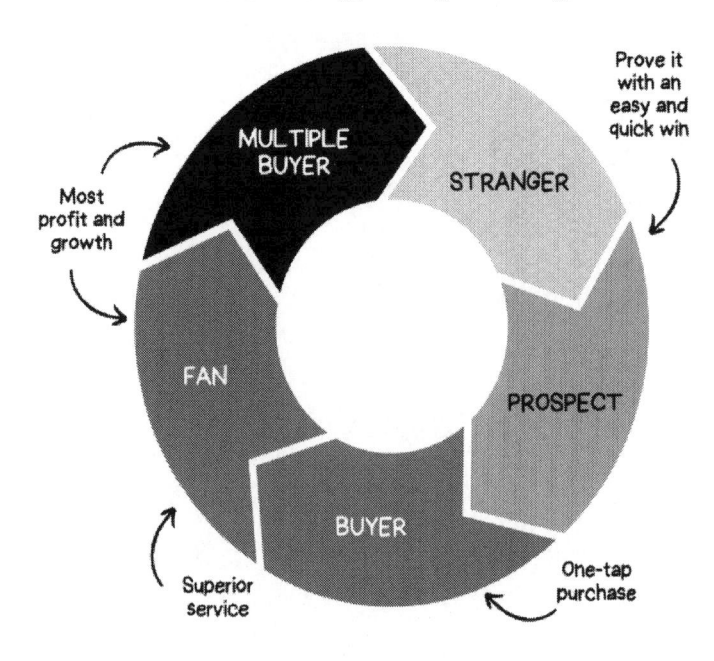

- STRANGER — Prove it with an easy and quick win
- PROSPECT — One-tap purchase
- BUYER — Superior service
- FAN
- MULTIPLE BUYER — Most profit and growth

Step 3: Automated messages to increase engagement

This is how you make more sales while you sleep.

The best thing about the "Prompt - Publish - Profit" model is - when you're not in build mode, it's passive, and its exponential - the bigger you build it, the bigger it continues to grow on its own.

Compare this to a business where you sell one-off high ticket, and as soon as you step out of operations or stop ads the whole thing comes crashing down.

The next step are automated messages that make your audiobook so sensational, it makes regular audiobooks seem like something from stone ages.

Imagine listening to your favorite audiobook and right when the author mentions a website, the details are texted to you.

Or finishing a really good audiobook and the author messages you and inviting you onto a call to discuss how this solution fits into your life.

The possibilities are endless, all because you're engaging your listener to take action.

It is not hard. It's not confusing. Especially if you follow a process, which is simpler than you think, and...

The process goes like this...

Step one, you create your book with the help of AI. The second step is to publish your audiobook in an afternoon, turning it into your automated selling machine. Then the third and final step is profit.

Those are the three steps you need: Prompt, publish and profit.

THE PROFIT PATH™

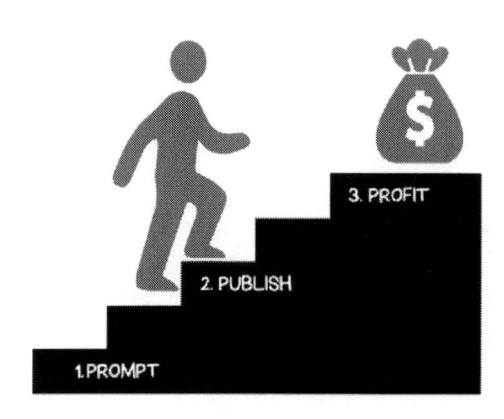

[Figure: A person climbing steps labeled "1. PROMPT", "2. PUBLISH", "3. PROFIT" toward a money bag.]

Automation does all the work for you, leaving you more time to focus on what you love doing the most. But, as you probably know, persuasion is a delicate art. You have to know what to say and how to say it in order to keep your audience engaged and interested. And when it comes to profiting from your show, you can do it in a way that makes you appear "pitchy" or gimmicky, and as a result ruin your sales (and reputation).

Or you can use the proven process that I created and will make working with you seem like a gift from the Heavens above. I've helped hundreds of students make an average of $3,000 in their first week, even if they were starting from scratch.

I want to help you have that same success too because your success is my success. There's a second reason too. When I reveal my special partnership opportunity at the end of this book (spoiler alert: it's a game changer), I hope you'll be so impressed that you'll want to take your business to the next level and shorten your time to success by working together with me and my team.

> **PRO TIP:** The more action you take throughout this guide, the more profits you'll make now, and partnering with me and my team will be virtually free.

Here's what I need from you–an implementation mindset. Implementation is key because nothing pains me more than giving you the solution that took me years to figure out just to discover years later you still have the same problem you have today. And sadly after I gave you the solution to solve it on a silver platter. Honestly, that hurts.

I want you to have an implementation mindset when you read this. It's not enough to just understand the solutions I'm sharing - you need to put them into action in order to see results.

Like Kiana Danial, for example. She's one of my friends and one of our first customers at Hiro. She has a talent for explaining investment to people who aren't great at math, and she implemented what I'm sharing here today. As a result, she hit her first million after adding audio to her business. And two years later, her business was earning over ten million dollars in sales!

So when you read this, I want you to think in terms of results and actions, not just intellect. And whenever you see something that excites you, take action on it. I'll provide you with small, easy-to-implement actions after each section to help you along the way.

I'm gonna give you my very best here, and all I ask in return is that you commit to putting what you learn into action. Can we make that happen? Will you take some massive action and make the most of this training? I sure hope so, because together, we can achieve some seriously awesome things.

Make the commitment now. Join our private Facebook group at https://facebook.com/groups/superhiros. Or you can reach out to me on social media and say,"Yes, I'm all in!" **Say it out loud right now.** I don't care if you're sitting in your living room or Starbucks right now, it doesn't matter. Say, "Yes."

ACTION STEPS

1. Join the Super Hiro Group (https://facebook.com/groups/superhiros)
2. Create an introduction post saying "I'm all in!"
3. Say it out loud as well (nothing is stronger than belief!)
4. That's it! See how easy it is?

UP NEXT

In the next chapter, I'm going to show you how to create use artificial intelligence to help write your book for you. No more spending months battling writers block. Instead, you'll learn how to turn all your expertise into money quickly and easily. So keep reading and get ready to start making money in minutes, not months.

CHAPTER 4: Prompt

From Writer's Block To Book In Record Time with ChatGPT

Okay, let's be real - writing a book is no joke. It's hard work and can take a crap-ton of time, especially when you're dealing with that pesky thing called writer's block. Trust me, I know all about it. So my claim that you can do this in record time might have you scratching your head.

When I was writing my first book, *"Idea to iPhone,"* I struggled more than I ever had with any app or software I'd created. I was battling with writer's block left and right, and no matter what I did, I just couldn't get the words to flow.

So when it came to writing this guide, I wasn't having any of it. And let's just say that hiring a professional writer didn't exactly go as planned - they were weeks late and the quality wasn't what I was hoping for.

So there I was, back at square one, wondering how the heck I was ever gonna get my book out into the world. That's when I discovered ChatGPT.

So, on a beautiful snowy day, I sat down to give it a try. And guess what was on in the background? The Argentina vs. Netherlands World Cup match. I mean, talk about motivation.

Well, let me tell you — using AI to write my book ended up being a total game changer. Not only was the process faster and more efficient, but the quality of the end result was off the charts.

But it's not all about the technology. To really succeed at writing a book using AI, you need to have a solid understanding of how the book formula works. How to touch the human spirit.

In this chapter, I'll spill the beans on how ChatGPT helped me overcome my struggles and write my book. More importantly, I share my secret formula based on books that have seriously changed the game so you can have their magic to your own work.

> **FUN FACT:** On average, it may take a full-time writer about six months to a year to write a book

My Binge-Like-Netflix Formula™

If you want to avoid putting your audience to sleep and instead position yourself as the expert that everyone's dying to hire, you need a formula. I've spent hours upon hours studying webinars, world class speeches, and best-selling books, and I've come up with a formula that works like a charm for both audiobooks and printed books.

This formula is the key to engaging your audience, getting your message across, and turning you into the go-to expert in your field. So pay attention, because this is the secret sauce that's gonna take your writing to the next level and help you achieve the kind of success you've always dreamed of.

In fact, this formula is one of my specialities and why I got into audio in the first place. When you create an audiobook like this, closing calls are more like, "Let's get your credit card and onboard you." Instead of dealing with hours of objections, having to speak to their spouse and wanting time to think about it. Let's break it down, step by step.

First, let me ask you this. Is it possible for you to give your ideal audience your best tactics, with all your best strategies and get zero cents as a result?

I've seen this many, many times. Coaches and experts saying, "I'm going to reveal everything I do in my business." And as a result, they see zero dollars and zero cents in their bank account. Why is this?

I discovered that there are three levels to sharing your expertise and becoming known as the best in your field. And when you deliver at that top level, you're known as the best and people will line up to work with you.

The first level is the method we just discussed, where you reveal all your secrets, tactics and systems and seldom leads to sales. The second level is getting your audience to have epiphanies and ideas, which is better than level one, but still isn't enough to convince them to buy from you. The third level is the most powerful and effective - it's where your audience adopts a new identity that positively changes their behavior. The key word here is *behavior*.

THREE LEVELS OF TEACHING

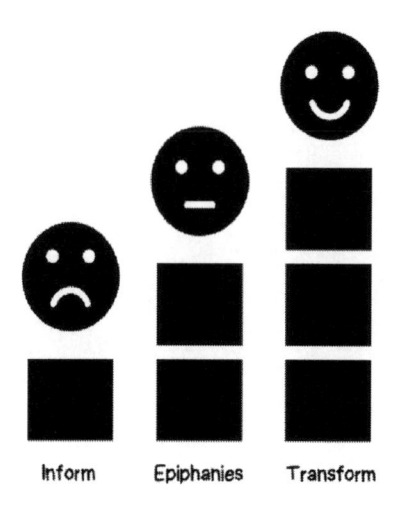

Inform　　Epiphanies　　Transform

By focusing on this third level, you can effectively empower your audience to confidently take action and buy from you. The real question becomes, how do you create a positive change in their behavior as a result of what you teach them?

Does the phrase "create value" ring a bell with you? So often we hear that to get rich, we need to create value. Well, what does that mean? Here's my definition that I'd love to share with you.

Creating value is when your listener gains insights in a way that they see themselves in a new way and go about life differently.

Here's how we create value in your book. If they were scared before and now they're confident, that's value. If they felt hopeless, and you gave them hope, my friend is extremely valuable. If they were confused, and you give them clarity. That's value. If they felt shame, and you replaced it with inner love, that is huge value.

That's what we want to accomplish with our content. Content done, right is this: **You say less, but you have a bigger impact.**

How do you do that?

Step 1: List The Top Problems You Solve

You want to sell the problem you solve, not talk about the product that you have. When you do this, you not only change their behavior, but also provide them with relief that someone understands them. Before I even hit record, I pull out a piece of paper and draw a line down the middle. On the left side of the line, I list the key problems that my audience is facing.

For example, if you're a health coach, problems might be feeling overwhelmed and unsure if they can stick to your program. They probably tried dozens of programs before, but never felt like they could truly commit to them. This can make it difficult to trust that your program will be any different. Part of your book focuses on solving that problem.

You could be a lawyer and your audience is scared to spending thousands on a long, drawn-out lawsuit that only brings stress. You might have an ads agency and prospects are concerned that ad costs will eat into their profits too much.

Knowing your audience's doubts, insecurities, and worries not only positions you as an expert, but can be an instant trust builder. Have you ever tried talking to friends or family about a problem, but they just didn't understand. Then someone comes along and can articulate the problem even better than you can? It's such a relief! By showing that you understand their struggles, they let out a big sigh of relief.

WHAT STOPS YOUR DREAM CUSTOMER FROM TAKING ACTION?

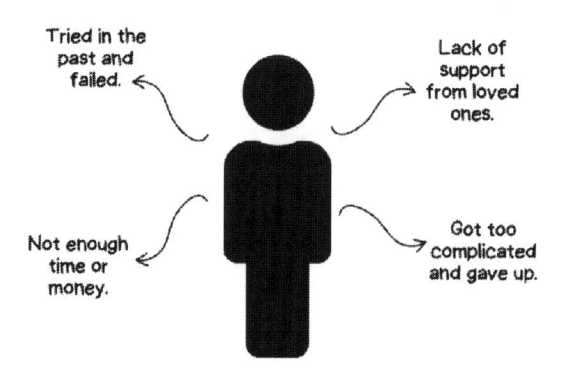

- Tried in the past and failed.
- Lack of support from loved ones.
- Not enough time or money.
- Got too complicated and gave up.

Step two: Match the problem to your solutions

First, discover your audience's biggest concerns and objections and list them on one side of the page. And then, on the other side, write the your solution that would overcome those objections or dispel the doubt. For example, the problem is "I'm a parent and don't have the time to learn all of this" becomes my solution, "How to learn everything while waiting for your kid at soccer practice."

Don't worry about the titles just yet. We will let artificial intelligence write those for us if we aren't sure what they should be.

> **PRO TIP:** If you want your book to really hit home with your audience, try using their own words to describe their problems. One of the best ways to do this is by actually talking to them and gathering their thoughts and experiences firsthand. Rather than relying on AI to try and

> capture their perspective, take the time to really listen and understand what they're going through. This will make your book that much more powerful and resonant.

The Perfect Audiobook Formula

This framework is vastly different from what you hear on webinars, challenges, or workshops. This framework is specifically designed for books - audiobooks and printed ones. You can use it for any speaking or teaching event that you attend, but be careful. It's going to create super fans.

ANATOMY OF A HIGH CONVERTING AUDIOBOOK

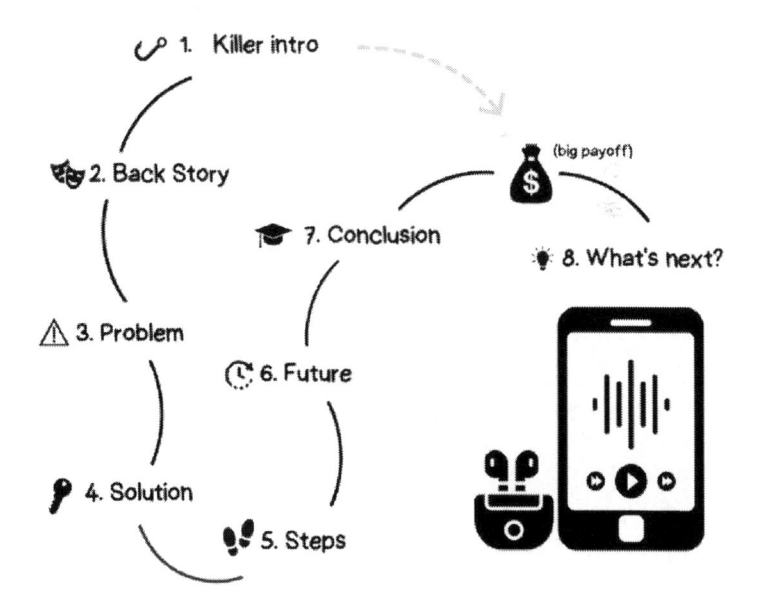

1. Killer intro
2. Back Story
3. Problem
4. Solution
5. Steps
6. Future
7. Conclusion (big payoff)
8. What's next?

53

First, we gotta hook them with a killer introduction that clearly states the payoff for listening all the way through. Next, we share a short story about how we discovered this system or someone who used it and had mad success. Then, we lay out our step-by-step process for achieving that same sweet outcome, so they can see a clear vision and strategy. After that, we do a quick recap to transition to the close, which is basically inviting them to work with us or buy our thing. Now, if all this seems overwhelming, don't sweat it. Sometimes we get all addicted to complexity, but don't fall into that trap. Once you have a recipe to follow, it becomes super simple.

Introduction

Let's start with the introduction. Here's the challenge with the introduction. You only have one chance to make a first impression. You have nine seconds, you can either dazzle or dull, inspire or annoy make money or cost you money. Nine seconds. Like a fine thoroughbred, you must start strong out of the gate.

Now here's what an ideal introduction accomplishes. It grabs your audience's attention and make them wanna binge listen. It should communicate that something special is about to go down that's gonna solve a problem that's been hurting your audience like crazy, and it should hold within it the promise that the future is bright and you're gonna help them make it a reality.

But most introductions don't accomplish even half of that. That's where I come in - I'm gonna hand you the golden ticket to never having a dull intro again. All my intros aim to do the following:

Hook the reader with a compelling personal story, a big outcome they'll get from finishing the book, shocking facts, uncommon beliefs and an amazing discovery. You also want to share how the future will be much better than the present.

Build authority by quickly sharing your accomplishments, name dropping, and testimonials and success stories.

State exactly who this book is for and who the book is not for. Call out internal desires and remove present pain, then expand. For example, "Are you tired of...", "Do you want more..." and "Are you ready for ..."

Deal with objections upfront and address their skepticism. For example "If you are concerned with X, the answer is Y." I repeat this for every objection the reader has.

How this book is different by giving them at least three solid reasons. I like one reason to be about my system. One reason to be about internal beliefs they have such as their skills or capabilities. And then one regarding external beliefs such as time.

Price and value of what you are sharing. How much will it make them, save them, change their lives? What do your clients pay you to get similar results?

Guidance on how to read this book. Do you want them to take action after each chapter? Should the reader commit to actions? Are you going to help them? Are you going to text them? Let them know.

Commit and celebrate their actions. The reader's actions lead to wins both big and small. When this happens, their doubts are replaced with confidence. Their fear is replaced with confidence. And their old identity is replaced with a new one.

Open loop to the next topic. This is how Netflix gets you to binge watch an entire season of a show in an afternoon. And this is how you get you create a 'page-turner' out of your book. Your open loop should be so good that your audience is scratching their heads saying, "Wait, what?!?"

Your Story

This is your backstory, but it's also your listener's story. Read that again, because most people miss that power tip. The whole point of this section is for people to feel like they know you and you know them. You walked in their shoes. The more vulnerable you are, the more impact your story is gonna have on folks. And impact is what keeps people hooked, so we wanna create as much impact as possible.

Your backstory is your chance to really connect with your audience and show them that you get what they're going through. When you're vulnerable and open about your own struggles and challenges, it helps your audience to see that you're a real person, just like them. And here's the thing - if your audience doesn't feel a connection to your story, they won't take any kind of action. It's that simple.

So make sure you bring in "all the feels" this section. Be as vulnerable and authentic as possible. Share your story in a way that's real and relatable, and focus on the lessons you learned and the challenges you faced. Your audience needs to know that you've been through the same stuff they are. It builds trust which is a must if you want them to follow your guidance.

Bottom line - don't be afraid to be vulnerable in your backstory. It's this honesty and authenticity that'll make the biggest impact on your listeners and help you build a strong connection with them. And if you don't have that connection, they ain't gonna take any kind of action. So make it count.

I usually follow a simple outline:

- Tell a short story about your background, upbringing, or childhood.
- Share what your life was like before you discovered your concept, system or solution.
- Create an identity for that person who you were before (for example, *Doubtful Douglas*)
- Tell them HOW and WHY you started doing what you are doing now.
- Explain how your success has impacted your family and those around you. What good have you done in the world because of the success you've had?
- Create an identity for the person you are now that you have your new system (for example, *Do-It-Now Douglas*)
- Share any awards or accolades you've been given for being an expert in your field. Yes, toot your own horn and toot it loud.
- Why should they believe in you, belief in themselves, have full confidence and clarity they are on the right path
- Conclude by building hope for a future that is much better than the present
- Get the reader to commit to taking action so that they can have that better future
- Get the reader to commit to the new identity.

> **PRO TIP:** you want to Sell them on 4 things:
> - Right opportunity? (book)
> - Right person? (author)
> - Right time? (them)
> - right identity (old them vs new them)

Problem

Alrighty, let's talk about diving deep into the problem. Here's the deal - the more you know about the problem, the more you know about the solution. It's that simple. So if you wanna solve a problem and help your readers out, you gotta get all up in that problem. Know what I mean?

That means taking a deep dive into the history of the problem you're trying to solve. Figure out the backstory of the concept, topic, or idea you want to relate to your readers. Write a chapter all about the history, the current situation, and the depth of the issues caused by this problem. It's all about getting to the heart of the matter and understanding what's really going on.

And let me tell you, this is important stuff. If you don't really understand the problem you're trying to solve, you ain't gonna have a clue about the solution. So take the time to do your research, dig deep, and get a real handle on what's going on. It'll be worth it in the end, I promise.

Solution

Okay, now let's talk about your unique solution. You gotta make sure your method stands out from the rest. So why is yours different? What have people tried in the past? What pains have they encountered? And most importantly, what does the future look like using your solution? These are all important questions to consider when it comes to your unique solution.

To really drive this point home, share stories about what people have tried in the past and the pains they've encountered. What hasn't worked for them? What's left them feeling frustrated and stuck? By highlighting these issues, you can make it clear that your solution is the answer they've been looking for.

And don't forget to paint a picture of the future. How will things look once your readers have implemented your solution? What kind of transformation can they expect? To really drive this home again, share a story about the future outcome. Help your readers see themselves in that picture, and they'll be more likely to take action.

Nothing brings an audience together and builds loyalty like having a common enemy. But we're not talking about a person here, we're talking about an idea, organization, or system. Something that your readers can rally against and feel united in their opposition to.

This is where your solution comes in. Make it clear how important it is and how "they" - whoever "they" might be - don't want your readers to know about it. Play up the idea that your solution is the secret weapon that's gonna help your readers triumph over their common enemy.

And to really drive the point home, top it off with a quote from someone your audience admires. Someone who speaks to their values and beliefs, and who they look up to. This'll give your message even more weight and help your readers feel like they're part of a bigger movement.

Your Steps For Creating Change

Okay, it's time to reveal your unique steps for achieving the results your readers have been searching high and low for. First things first - talk about how you discovered this step. What was the process like? What challenges did you face? And most importantly, how did it change your life?

To really hammer home the impact of this step, talk about what life was like before you stumbled upon it. What pains were you experiencing? What was holding you back? And then contrast that with what life is like now, after you've implemented this step. Share a story about how great things are now, and help your readers see themselves in that same position.

And don't forget to create a common enemy here too. Why don't "they" - whoever "they" might be - want your readers to know about this step? How is your solution being kept a secret? Play up the idea that your readers are part of a bigger movement, fighting against the forces that are trying to keep them down.

Finally, make it crystal clear what the first thing your readers need to do is. What actions can they take right now to get started? Make it easy for them to take that first step, and you'll be well on your way to helping them achieve the results they've been dreaming of.

> **PRO TIP:** Rinse and repeat for each chapter of your steps

What the Future Holds

Alright, let's talk about helping your readers see themselves at the finish line. You know how all great athletes visualize themselves crossing the finish line before they even run the race? It's a powerful tool that increases their odds of success. And we want that for our readers too.

This is where you get to let your readers' imaginations run wild. Maybe they've been too scared to dream so big before. Maybe they didn't think it was possible for them. But now, with your help, they can clearly see a path to success. So let them envision themselves crossing that finish line.

To really drive this home, tell stories from your customers or clients. Use a variety of stories so you touch all kinds of readers. Paint a picture in their minds eye with as much detail as possible. Help them see themselves succeeding, and you'll increase their odds of actually making it happen.

So remember, just like great athletes visualize their success, you want to help your readers do the same. Use stories, paint a vivid picture, and help them see themselves at the finish line. Do all that, and you'll increase their chances of success.

Conclusion

First recap what you covered so far. This is important for a few reasons. First of all, it helps build on the momentum you've already established. By reminding your readers of what they've learned, you're helping to reinforce those key points. And let's be real - most people forget 90% of what they hear the first time around, so this is key.

As you recap, be sure to highlight the most important conclusions. I like to do this with a series of "yes" questions. By getting your readers to say "yes" over and over again, you're building momentum and setting the stage for the big "yes" - which, of course, is "yes, I will invest in your offer."

To really drive this home, fire off a series of "yes" questions one after the other. Things like:

- Was our time together thus far enjoyable for you?
- Have you also found it to be valuable?
- Do you now feel more comfortable with your ability to make money with your audiobook?
- Have you come up with some good ideas that you're already excited about implementing in your business?
- And is it fair to say that using these techniques will give you a significant advantage over your competition?

Pile on the the smaller "yeses" and your chances of a bigger "yes" later on becomes exponentially more powerful.

Now, before you move on to sharing your offer, you want to seed the idea in your readers' minds. One way to do this is by using a simple question like "You might be asking yourself, what's next?" Even if they weren't actually thinking this, you've just planted the seed and gotten them curious. And once you've got them wondering "what's next?", you can introduce your "Next Steps" - your offer.

Next Steps

Now that they finished the book, it's time to talk about how you can help them move forward with the solution that they desperately been seeking. While the entire point of this book was to get them to take action, it's important to keep this section brief. Pushing too hard can come across as desperate as they guy without a date on prom night. So be cool about it.

Offer a few options for moving forward, such as doing it on their own, working with your for additional help, hiring you to speak at an event, or reaching out to you for something else. If you have case studies, now is the time to share them. This will give your readers an idea of what it might be like to work with you and help them determine if they're a good fit.

Next, provide clear instructions on how to set up an appointment to explore the potential partnership further. This might include filling out a form, sending an email, or setting up a call. Make it easy for your readers to take that first step towards achieving the results they desire.

Of course, not everyone is going to be a good fit at this time. That's okay. In fact, it's important to be honest about this. If someone isn't ready to work with us yet, that's okay. Just provide some general advice and instruction for how they can continue to work on their problem on their own. Let them know that you're available to answer any questions and offer support, but also make it clear that you respect their decision if they decide not to move forward at this time.

Overall, the key is to be honest, transparent, and supportive. If you do that, you'll be able to build a strong connection with your readers rather than push them into something.

AI Writing Tools

There are various AI writing tools available on the market, each with its own unique features and capabilities so it can get overwhelming quick. One of my favorites and the one I used to write this book is ChatGPT which is currently free.

Other AI writing tools include Jasper.ai, Copy.ai, and Wordsmith, which uses machine learning algorithms to automate the writing process. These tools are incredibly simple to use, especially ChatGPT.

To use ChatGPT to write copy, follow these steps:

1. Open a web browser and go to the ChatGPT website. (https://chat.openai.com)
2. Create an account if you don't already have one.
3. Log in to your account and click on the "ChatGPT" button.
4. Type in a few words or phrases to get the opening for your book.
5. ChatGPT will respond with suggestions and ideas for your copy.
6. Keep talking to ChatGPT and it will continue to provide ideas and suggestions. For example, if the first response was dry, you can say "Make it funnier and something a 3rd grader understands."
7. Follow the quick start at the back of this guide for more suggestions.

That's it! ChatGPT makes it easy to write copy, even if you're not a professional writer. Just have a conversation with it and it will help you come up with ideas and words to use.

How To Train AI

The trick to getting AI to produce high quality copy is to "train" it first. Training AI to write for you involves giving it a lot of examples of writing that you like and then letting it try to generate its own sentences. This helps it learn how to "speak" like you.

First, gather a bunch of examples of writing, such as articles, stories, or poems in the tone of voice you want. We then feed these examples to the AI, one sentence at a time.

Next, the AI uses what it has learned from the examples to try to generate its own sentences. It does this by looking at the words that have been used so far and using them to make a guess about what the next sentence might be.

If the AI's sentence is good, we let it keep going. But if the sentence is not good, we tell it what is wrong and have it try again. Over time, the AI gets better and better at generating sentences that make sense and sound natural.

Finally, after practice, the AI becomes very good at generating its own writing and can produce high-quality texts on its own. This is how we train AI to write for us in the tone of voice that sounds like you.

> **BONUS:** A list of prompts are provided in the back of this book.

Real live example

What I entered into AI for instructions:

write a short story about how a woman discovered how to lose weight while eating hamburgers and shakes and sitting on the coach

What AI created:

Samantha had struggled with her weight for as long as she could remember. She had tried every diet and exercise program out there, but nothing seemed to work for her. She was frustrated and felt like she was running out of options.

One day, she stumbled upon an advertisement for a weight loss program that promised she could lose weight while eating hamburgers and shakes and sitting on the couch. It sounded too good to be true, but she was desperate and decided to give it a try.

To her surprise, the program actually worked! She was able to eat all of her favorite foods, and still lose weight. She even had energy to spare and was able to keep up with her busy schedule.

Samantha was thrilled with her newfound success, and started sharing her story with friends and family. Soon, she had a whole community of people following her program and seeing amazing results.

She realized that this program was not only effective, but also sustainable. She no longer felt like she was depriving herself or sacrificing her happiness to lose weight. She was finally able to enjoy her life and feel confident in her own skin.

Samantha was grateful for the program that had changed her life, and was excited to continue helping others achieve their weight loss goals. She was proof that it was possible to lose weight and still enjoy the things you love.

> **NOTE:** You don't have to use AI to write your content. You can use our formula to create your book and record it. Or you can find materials you already have and use existing content to create your show.

Key Points:

- If you really want your audiences to get results, don't just inform, but rather transform.

- Our "Binge-Like-Netflix" formula is unique to both books and audiobooks and isn't available anywhere else. It's a formula crafted form years of researching and studying countless webinars, world-class speakers and best-selling books.

- The better you guide AI, the better your results will be. So take the time to understand the problem you're solving and that will help AI help your writing.

- AI is a tool for your first draft. Just like AI images often need fixing in an editing tool like Photoshop, AI writing will need some editing too.

- Use stories throughout your book, not just in your backstory section. Stories are what build trust and without it, your audience won't take action.

HOMEWORK

1. Using the prompts at the back of this book, create your first draft of your book.

2. Copy and paste everything into a Google document.

3. Get the first draft done and then go back again and fix areas that need improving.

UP NEXT

> In the next section, I'll show you how you can publish your show in record time by turning it into a list building audiobook that sells your services for you.

CHAPTER 5: Publish

How to free yourself from the system and publish your audiobook in minutes (not months)

We already covered why audio is a secret powerhouse to connecting with your audience in a deeper way. When you read your own words out loud, you have the opportunity to infuse your book with your own personality and energy. And let's be real - that's something you can't get from a traditional, printed book.

Audiobooks are also ten times faster and less expensive to produce. Think about it- there's no editing or formatting involved, and you get to read everything you wrote out loud first, which helps ensure that your book flows smoothly. So let's use what you created and turn on your Automated Selling Machine.

More than that, we're going to take your audiobook game to the champion level. I've got a secret for you: **interactive audiobooks are the future.** Let's walk you through this new frontier of publishing.

Your Automated Selling Machine

I know that for some people, the thought of using technology can be a little intimidating. I'm here to help you every step of the way. And if you're worried that creating an your Automated

Selling Machine is going to add even more to your already full plate, let me assure you that it's actually going to do the opposite. By using automation, you'll be able to save time and reduce the amount of manual labor required to run your business.

I'm guessing that you probably created a website or funnel to collect emails in exchange for a PDF. Or maybe you spent months building out a challenge like I did. But let me ask you this: did the process end up taking you way longer than you thought? What you hoped would take you a few days ended up being months. Maybe it's still not launched.

Before I started using Hiro, I did things the old way. It's what I knew and what I had been taught to do. And I'm sure you've seen the same thing - people selling old, complicated methods that require huge budgets and teams to make them work. But the truth is, those methods are outdated and don't work for most people.

The Cost Of Outdated Models

What many "gurus" boasting about six and seven figure launches aren't telling you is that they spent almost half that in expenses, sometimes more. They're selling you on a model that is nearly impossible for most businesses to replicate without a massive budget and high quality team. I bought into all of it.

When I was running my challenge, I was out of pocket a good $23,000 before I even launched. And it would take months to pull it all together. If it didn't work out, I would lose out on 10's of 1000's of dollars.

THE HIDDEN COSTS OF OUTDATED SYSTEMS

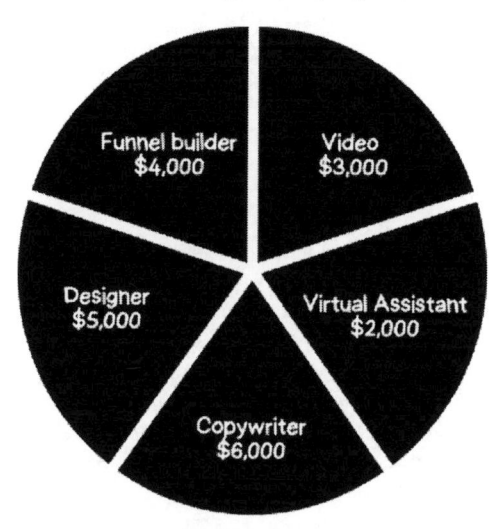

- Funnel builder $4,000
- Video $3,000
- Virtual Assistant $2,000
- Copywriter $6,000
- Designer $5,000

*over $23,000 without counting ads

I was betting the farm. It's stressful, tough and confusing. It's why I was a zombie sitting at the dinner table with my kids every night. But that's how everybody's been doing it for the last ten years.

Let's start with the right tools. Because, to automate all this so it's one-tap simple, you're going to need the tools that will build the foundation of your business. The main tool is your audio distribution software (of course) is Hiro.fm.

With less tech and the right tools, you'll have less things that can break. If you're using complicated systems, not only do they take money out of your pocket, they all have to fit together and if one little thing breaks, the whole thing breaks.

HIRO'S ALL-IN-ONE SOLUTION

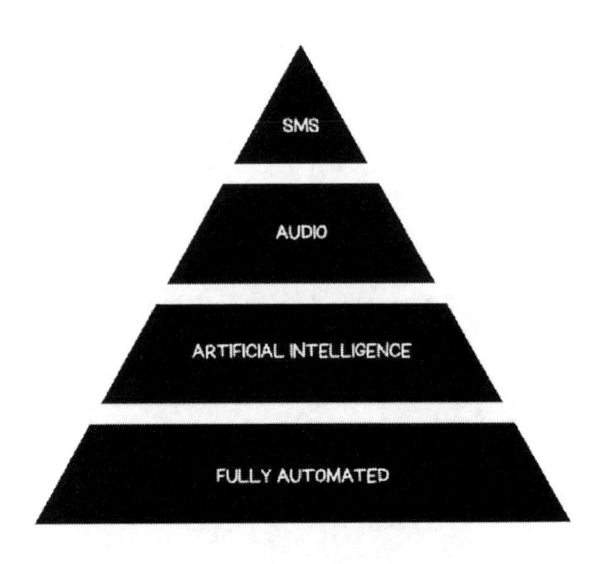

- SMS
- AUDIO
- ARTIFICIAL INTELLIGENCE
- FULLY AUTOMATED

PRO TIP: Complexity fails, simplicity scales

When you start leveraging audio, specifically Hiro, you'll be harnessing one of the biggest, newest, secret weapons to hit marketing in decades.

Let me show you why. I'll put together the entire Automated Selling Machine system from scratch in 3 minutes. To watch, point your phone camera to this code and click on the link or go to https://hiro.fm/quickstart:

Before I started using Hiro, I can't even tell you how many hours I wasted trying to create videos, websites, pages, and funnels. It was so frustrating and time-consuming. But with Hiro, I've been able to save all those hours and get my message out there in a fast and effective way. In fact, I've been able to create a new product in just ten minutes!

Even if I didn't make any money from the Hiro software itself, I more than doubled my profits by using it in my coaching business. And I have to give a shout-out to my team, who are so passionate about your mission and have worked hard to make Hiro better and easier to use every day.

You'll notice every day that the Hiro Team is making the software easier and more powerful. You can literally imagine a new product, and ten minutes later have it out there for people to buy.

> " I don't know how many times I tried to create a course of my own with all the steps. This was by far the quickest and most simple way to create a digital product. It literally took me minutes to set it up. "

ANGIE MINUCCI, COURSE CREATOR

PRO TIP: You can see more stories at https://hiro.fm/review

How To Get A Massive Subscriber List With One Word

I remember when I first started Hiro, I was so excited to build my email list. I spent days creating a beautiful PDF download and put it up on our website for people to grab for free. I thought for sure that I would get a flood of emails from people eager to get my best tactics. But as the days turned into weeks, and then months, I only received a handful of emails. I was disheartened but determined.

I decided to try something different and invested in some advertising to promote my PDF download. This brought in a few more emails, but it was still a trickle compared to what I had hoped for. It seemed like no matter what I did, most people just weren't interested in entering their email address.

It wasn't until I did some research that I learned a shocking fact: **the average conversion rate for free opt-ins is just 1-3%.** That means that out of 100 visitors to my website, only 1-3 of them would actually take the time to enter their email address. It was a harsh reality to face, but it also motivated me to find a better way to build my email list.

Want to know a secret to insane conversion rates? It's called SMS keyword optin, and it's a game changer. Studies show that SMS messaging has a conversion rate of around 45%, which is way higher than email marketing or social media ads. That's because SMS is a super personal form of communication that's hard to ignore. By using SMS keyword opt-in, you can grab your audience's attention and turn them into customers like a boss.

If you want to easily build up a massive subscriber list, all you have to do is use the power of SMS keyword opt-in. It's super simple to set up: just choose a keyword that's easy to remember and spell, and share it everywhere you can think of - podcasts, videos, social media profiles, email signatures, and more. When someone texts that keyword to your dedicated number, they'll get access to your audiobook. With this tactic, you'll be able to grow your subscriber list in no time, with minimal effort on your part.

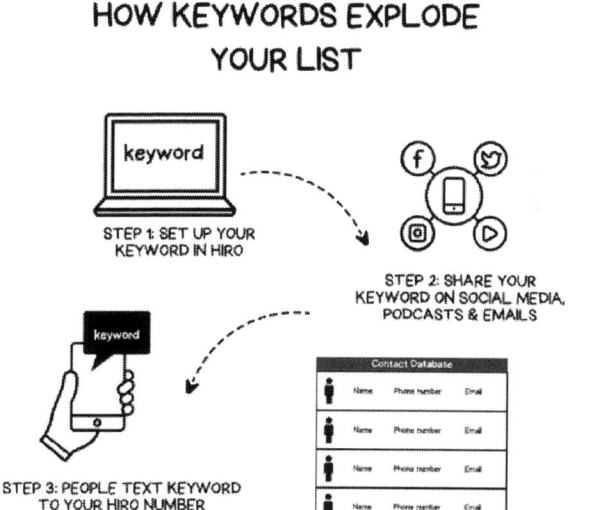

HOW KEYWORDS EXPLODE YOUR LIST

STEP 1: SET UP YOUR KEYWORD IN HIRO

STEP 2: SHARE YOUR KEYWORD ON SOCIAL MEDIA, PODCASTS & EMAILS

STEP 3: PEOPLE TEXT KEYWORD TO YOUR HIRO NUMBER

STEP 4: YOU GET A MEGA LIST

The Fortune Is in the Follow Up — How to Seal the Deal with Just Three Text Messages

My app, Gratitude Journal, survived over 13 years on the App Store when most apps fail after the first couple of months. To be honest, mine almost failed too. I was only making 69 cents on each customer who got my app. They could use my app for ten years and never pay me a single penny more, yet I was forever paying for their images and journal entries on my servers. It was a broken business model that nearly destroyed my business. I had to figure out how to increase my average customer value to stay alive.

Then one day I jumped on Amazon to buy some a Buzz Lightyear toy for my son. After adding it to my cart, Amazon showed me other products I might be interested. About $148 later, the answer to my app problem hit me. I knew how I could make more money from my customers.

I created my version of "Amazon Suggestion" in my Gratitude app. By adding a simple in-app notification, I was able to quickly 100x my profits by promoting my other products and services to existing customers.

NOTIFICATIONS SAVED MY APP

Whenever I hosted one of my online challenges or launched a new product, I used the notification to encourage my users to sign up. This helped me get hundreds of people to join my challenges without spending a single penny on advertising.

My clever use of in-app notifications not only helped me boost my average customer value, but it also got my podcast, *Radical Shift*, to the top of the charts and featured in magazines like Entrepreneur (right next to Tim Ferris and Oprah)!

Sometimes I would surprised my users with small gifts or ask to connect on social media too. Just like how the Clubhouse app exploded, notifications are key to insane growth without messing around with ads.

Creating Your Own Notifications

In this section of the guide, I will show you how to create a series of automated messages that will encourage your listeners to take action and purchase your product or book a call with you. This strategy lets you to bypass the frustrations of ads or email marketing and reach your audience directly, at the optimal time. It is simple and effective.

These magic messages are on autopilot and you only need a few messages to get results.

Plus, this approach can help you sidestep the problems caused by recent changes to Facebook and Apple's advertising policies. By keeping your audience within your own ecosystem, you can maintain control over your marketing efforts and make sure your message is delivered effectively-putting you in charge of your marketing.

Here's the exact setup and wording of these three magic messages, so you can start seeing results right away.

HOW TO STEAL YOUR COMPETITORS' TRAFFIC (& DECLARE VICTORY)

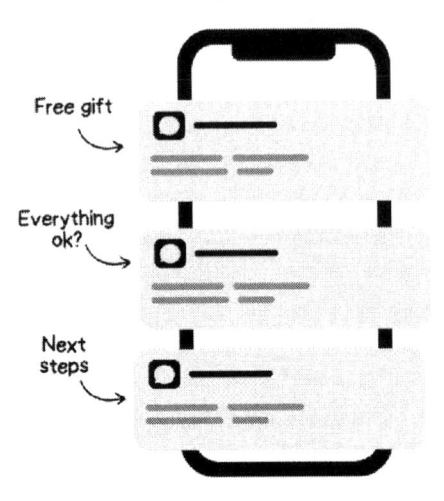

Free gift

Everything ok?

Next steps

Message One: The Gift

Have you ever felt compelled to help someone because she helped you in the past? This is known as the law of reciprocity, and it's a really powerful way to influence others and build trust.

An easy way to leverage the law of reciprocity is giving listeners a small gift-it could be a checklist, a spreadsheet, or something else that's useful to them. For example, when you listen to the audio version of this guide, I send you a free PDF workbook that helps you follow along. It's a simple gesture, but it goes a long way in making people feel grateful and indebted to you.

It's important that give your gift without expecting something in return. You honestly want your listeners to get results faster and your free gift will help them achieve that.

Message Two: "Everything okay?"

You can keep your listeners engaged and ensure they continue to listen to your podcast by sending them a message asking if everything is okay. This can be a great way to check in and show that you care.

Simply set up a message that sends automatically few days after they stop listening and asking if they need any help or support. You may be surprised at how many people respond and say that they were enjoying your audiobook but something came up. This little gesture can go a long way in keeping your audience coming back for more.

Message Three: "Next steps"

The third automatic message gives listeners direction on what they need do next to keep getting results even faster. This is when you can invite them to go further. Here are some suggestions for invitations:

- Watch a training
- Attend an event
- Purchase a product
- Book a call

At the end of my audiobook, I highlight the key takeaways and then send out a message saying, "Hey, I love people who invest in themselves and take action. I just got an opening in my calendar this week and would love to chat. Just pick a time that works for you. I hope this message helps you and I look forward to connecting with you soon!"

And that's it. Three messages. One is a gift. Two is, "Hey, are you okay?" And three is, "Do you want to book a call?"

You can do more messages than that. For instance, I gave my listeners of the audio version of this book a message with almost every chapter. You can do that as well. But you don't have to.

Instead of flooding your audience with messages, try guiding them with your automated messages. This will help you create a "trail to money" and make it easier for your audience to take action.

You can use AI to write your message.

Key Takeaways

- Record your audiobook before printing it so you can make sure that it flows and reads well

- Use that recording to create your Automatic Selling Machine by turning it into an audiobook that grows your list

- Adding automated messages to your audiobook increases engagement, makes it unique and allows you to connect with your readers in a way that you couldn't with Audible or other platforms.

- SMS text messages have a 99% open rate and are opened in the first 10 seconds of receiving them, compared to email which has an average of 17% open rate.

- You can give you audiobook away using a keyword opt-in or you can sell it with Hiro's no-code sales page.

Homework

1. **If you have first draft done, record it.** You can use your earbuds if that's the best mic you have and a free tool to remove the noise and enhance the audio quality (https://podcast.adobe.com/enhance)
2. **Create your cover art.** Canva is a free tool that you can use to create artwork for your audiobook. (https://canva.com)
3. Log into your Hiro account and create your audiobook. Add the title, description and cover art.
4. Share your show in the Super Hiro group

Extra Credit:

1. Create your keyword for people to text and get access to your audiobook
2. Set up your three automated messages.
3. Add yourself as a listener and test it out!

You can follow the tutorials at https://hiro.fm/quickstart

Pro Tip

How to create world class marketing materials to promote your audiobook:

1. Add yourself as a listener to your audiobook
2. Play your show in the Hiro mobile app
3. Take a screenshot of your show
4. Upload the screenshot to Canva
5. Create a new social media post in Canva with a Phone photo holder

6. Add the screenshot of your show to the Canva post so it looks like it's playing on a phone
7. Add earbuds or headphones so they know it's audio
8. Download and use in your social media posts, profile headers, emails and marketing

[Call out If you do run into problems, here's what you can do. You can reach out to our support staff via email at hello@hiro.fm. They're there to help you. You can also reach out to the Super Hiro community in our Facebook group. Both of the links will be in the show and guide notes.]

Up Next

Before launching your show, I'm going to show you how to get listeners. That's right - even before you've created a single episode, you'll have people asking for your audiobook. And the best part is, I'm going to reveal how to do it with just one simple social media post. It doesn't matter how big your audience is - anyone can use this method to get more listeners for their audiobook. So keep reading!

CHAPTER 6: Profit

How to outsell the competition, even if they're industry giants

Now we get to the fun part. How you can turn your written words into cold, hard cash. You already know that, recording an audiobook is one of the fastest ways to do it.

Not only do you not have to worry about editing or formatting, but reading your work out loud is an absolutely must to making sure it flows smoothly and makes sense to your listeners. Plus, the demand for audiobooks is booming at the same rate physical books is declining. More and more people are turning to audiobooks, and as a business owner, you can tap into that demand and start making money from your audiobook.

But you're not just creating the audiobook and hoping for the best. There are strategies you can use to maximize your profits and make sure your audiobook is a success. In this chapter, we'll go over some of the ways you can profit from your audiobook, including how to price it, how to promote it, and how to make the most of each sale. So buckle up and get ready to start making money from your words!

Ways To Profit

Selling your book and audiobook is just one way to make money. In fact, it's not even the best way to profit. Your profits are from the higher priced items you sell to your audience the more they engage with you. These can be premium services, masterminds, events, or other products.

You don't want your readers to feel like they've been tricked into getting your book only to find out it's just a sales pitch in disguise. That's why it's so important to make sure your book is packed with value. Your readers should be able to get results on their own just by reading your book. Of course, hiring you or purchasing your products can help them get those results even faster, but the point is that they should still feel like they've gained something valuable from your book.

Buying Is Like Winning A Prize (Steal This Script)

People who read your book still need to know if they're the right fit for your product or service. Give them step by step directions and clarify exactly what will happen in the next steps. A confused buyer is a no buyer.

"If you're the right fit, here's how we can move forward with a solution and partner."

If you offer a service, state working together is a partnership. This lets them know you have skin in the game. Now if you have testimonials, this is the perfect time to use them and here's how.

> "And just to give you an idea to determine if you're a right fit or not, here's some of the people that we've worked with who were the perfect fit for us to help them achieve an outcome."

Then share your case studies and stories of people you helped in the past with the same sort of outcome.

> "If you feel you're the right fit, here's what you need to do."

Explain in a few sentences that you're gonna give them instructions on how to set up an appointment to take one step forward to explore the potential partnership further. I also like tell them what to expect on the call.

> "Essentially two things happen at the end of these calls. One is we feel good about a win-win situation. And then we come up with the best way to proceed forward with that in a professional agreement. Or one of us, or maybe both of us decides is that at this time, it doesn't make sense. Which is fine. If it doesn't make sense to you, then it won't make sense to me. But if it doesn't make sense to you, then we're not gonna do business together right now we can remain friends. No hard feelings, no obligation on either side."

This lowers their guard about getting on a call with a pushy sales person and wasting their time. We want these calls to be like onboarding calls rather than a sales call, and the more they come in feeling confident about their choices, the easier that is to accomplish.

> *"However, if you're not comfortable yet, consider this. Are you somebody who's looking for this solution? Do you suppose it's important to get a second set of eyes on your problem? Does it make sense to have an objective party explore your problem further and then use that to determine what we should do together? And if so, then use the information on how to set an appointment with us."*

I like to give them a few questions that if they say yes to them, then they should contact you because it's highly likely you'll be able to help them.

And then "not yet" people. This is important. I didn't say "yes" or "no". I said "yes" or "not yet". The implication is maybe one day.

> *"If you're not a right fit yet, here are the three things I recommend that you do that will put you in a position that if you then want to partner with us. If you do all these things, then if you decide to come back and, and partner with us great. And if you don't fantastic as well, just let me know your results."*

This implies that the reader will still work with you one day. Then give them some simple steps they can take that will allow them to work with you soon.

You're not feeling like a sleazy salesman when you try to invite your readers to join a call or purchase your products and your readers feel welcome and excited about the opportunity to work with you or buy your products. By following these simple steps, you'll be able to create a connection with your readers that is authentic, genuine, and profitable.

> **PRO TIP:** You're not in the sales business, you're in the customer for life business. The sooner you realize that, the sooner your business will grow.

A Single Social Media Post That Can Attract 100s of Listeners

Once people get to this point they start asking me, *"Now that I've created this audiobook, where are all these alleged people, who will be my listeners, where are they coming from?"*

Most likely, you're committing this very small, yet major mistake, which is possibly robbing you blind. I'm going to fix all that with a little trick that will get you listeners and kill the number one enemy in your business – procrastination.

I discovered that most people trying to make money are not going to finish the product. They're never going to launch. I've watched this happen over and over in the marketplace and many struggle for years, costing them an absolute fortune.

When you have a half-finished book or course that are just gathering dust on your hard drive, it's a waste of time, energy, and money. And I know I'm not the only one who has a few of those – I bet you do too. We all look at what other people have created and think that we have to make ours better, so we spend months tweaking and wondering if it will ever be good enough for people to buy. But we're stuck in a cycle of procrastination and perfectionism – we wait for the perfect moment to start, and then we try to make it even better. And of course, there's always the temptation of shiny new ideas that can derail our progress. Raise your hand, if it sounds familiar (yes, you, sitting in Starbucks. Hand up!)

But it doesn't have to be this way. With one simple post, you can break out of this cycle and launch products that people will love. And that's what we're going to show you in this section. So let's get started and turn those unfinished products into something that can help people and make you money.

It's not rocket science. You can't even procrastinate or perfect it because it is crazy simple.

This is the post:

THE HAND RAISER POST

> I just recorded a private podcast sharing how to go from 0-$250K in a year with no funnel, list or ads.
> Who wants it?
>
> 291 comments

This post alone has gotten me hundreds of listeners and dozens of clients. This is called a "hand raiser post" and assignment is simple. Go onto social media and create a simple Facebook post just like this one. Here's the formula:

"I just explained in an audiobook, the fastest way [big result] in [time period] without [things they don't want or have]. Do you want access?"

I remember the first time I used the "hand raiser" post. It was like a magic bullet - it got me 100 listeners and it took out procrastination and perfectionism before they even knew what hit them. And those pesky "shiny objects" didn't stand a chance.

This is why this single post is so powerful. It calls on your ideal audience because it speaks directly to problem they're working on right now and a simple solution they can see working for them. Very important key to making this work is this: instead of just focusing on the benefits–because that's what everybody does, they brag about all the benefits – but what prospects want is for you to eliminate their pain.

Pain can be giving up their favorite foods, learning how to do sales calls, dealing with tech, or having to get a spouse to agree. These are just a few examples, but there are many other things that can hold people back. It's important to identify what those are for your audience and address them in your post. Think of at least two things are preventing people from taking action and achieving their goals and eliminate them in your process and you will strike gold.

If you're a lawyer, your post could be "I just explained in an audiobook the fast way to build a rock solid case that will crush your opponent without investing in thousands of legal fees upfront." (If you're a lawyer and you make that audiobook, send me access ok? Thanks!)

Don't overcomplicate this. Remember, complexity fails. Just open Facebook right now and make your post. **Yes, RIGHT NOW! Set down this guide, open your phone and write that post.**

If people leave comments and respond then fantastic! You just made yourself a whole bunch of cash! Congratulations! What's even more amazing is that you can no longer procrastinate creating your show. You have to do it. Your feet are to the fire.

If you don't, you're just saying no to a bunch of money. And why would you do that? You have to hate money to not spend a few days creating your audiobook and letting those fine folks know you have the answer to their prayers.

What if nobody responds? What if your post only one like and it's from your mom? To that I say "Fantastic! That's awesome too!"

And you might be thinking "Wait ... what? Fantastic? How could that be?"

It's fantastic because you just saved yourself from creating a book that no one is interested in. Aren't you glad you found out now? It's far easier to recover from a post that didn't get any comments than a launch that didn't get any sales.

Are you still reading this and haven't posted on Facebook yet? Do your post today. Can you do that? Will you promise me that you'll try this out? I don't think that's too much to ask.

When you make your Facebook post, make sure it's "public" so anyone can see it. And then share your post in the Super Hiro Facebook group.

The Steps:

1. Create the post and make it public
2. Share your post in the Hiro FB group link so we can all love on it

When you commit to my "hand raiser post", you're doing yourself a favor because you get out of your way. **Instead you get to make money, which is how this game should be played.**

This guide isn't "let me show you a perfect way to do it." Let me show you a way that's gonna make you as much money as soon as possible in one setting. Like my friend Victoria, one of my favorite people in the world, is incredibly smart and successful. She just said, "Okay, let's do it."

She didn't second guess. She just went out and made a post. She wrote, "This is hot off the press and finally here. This year, I got the guidance to share something new. And it's a gift to all of you. It's a private podcast. So yesterday, I just recorded an intuitive reading for business and life success. And I just finished uploading it, who wants it?"

Victoria messaged me later after she sent it ou saying she got a whole bunch of people who wanted it and, "I closed another $12,000 client on the phone just now. I am so happy."

> **PRO TIP:** Share your 'hand raiser post' on Facebook, Instagram, YouTube, LinkedIn, your email list too

What to do when people reply to your post

When someone shows interest in your audiobook by replying to one of your posts, it's crucial that you send them a direct message to thank them and give them access to your show. Trust me, this is way more effective than just sharing a link or opt-in keyword in your post. By sending a personal message, you come across as more relatable and friendly. Plus, you can learn more about the person and have the chance to follow up with them. This little tip alone can boost your conversion rates by a whopping 10x or more. So don't be afraid to send a personal message - it'll make a huge difference in your success.

> **PRO TIP:** You know what separates the top earners from the rest of the pack? Follow-up. That's right - even if someone says no to your offer, don't give up on them just yet. Keep checking in, because you never know when they'll be ready to say yes.

5 Effortless Audiobook Profits

These are so simple, it's almost a crime! And will help our sales skyrocket.

1. **Sell the audiobook directly to consumers.** And the best part? You can sell your audiobook from the Hiro platform without even having to create a website, funnel, or sales page for it. Each show on the Hiro platform comes with a no-code sales page, so all you have to do is add a bit of description text and boom - you have a sales page!

2. **Offer the audiobook as a bonus or add-on product when someone purchases a related product or service.** For example, if you sell an online course, you can offer your audiobook as an additional product that your customers can purchase. This is sometimes called a "bump" and can range in price from a few dollars to a few hundred, depending on the price of your course. This is a super easy way to increase the average cart value (ACV) of your customers.

3. **Promote the audiobook to your email list or social media followers** and encourage them to purchase it. You can launch it at a special reduced price just for your insiders. Or bundle it with a free consulting call.

4. **Bundle the audiobook with a physical product, event or course and sell it as a package deal.** This is really powerful if you want to start people on a subscription service like a membership or software as a service (SaaS).

5. **Partner with people or organizations to promote the audiobook and earn a commission on each sale.** This is the fastest way to get a huge audience but can take time if you don't already have a relationship with people who have big audiences.

An Absolute Must If You're On TV, Radio or Presenting From Stage

It was a huge missed opportunity, and one that I vowed never to repeat. *The Tamron Hall Show* flew me to New York City to have me as a special guest. The topic was "Woman Who Disrupt By Creating Apps" and I was their main guest. I was so excited to share my app, Gratitude Journal, and hopefully get some sales.

There was just one problem. She didn't mention the full name of my app and with hundreds of gratitude apps on the App Store, I knew viewers won't be able to find it.

So, on the day of the airing, I jumped on The Tamron Hall Show's website and shared a link to my app. Hundreds of people grabbed it, but I couldn't help wondering how many missed out because they didn't visit the website.

A few weeks later, I was talking to a client who speaks at events all over the world, and he told me about this genius strategy he uses to build his email list. He tells his audience not to take notes or snap pictures of his slides while he's speaking, and instead promises to give them the notes and a recording of the entire presentation after he's finished. This way, everyone is fully focused on him during the talk. And then, when he's done, he tells them how they can get the recording and notes by texting a special keyword to his phone number. This way, he's able to capture the contact information of every single person who attended his presentation. It's such a smart, simple way to grow your email list.

Are you tired of wondering who's actually listening when you're on stage, TV, or radio? Well, here's a little trick for you: offer your audiobook as a free gift for anyone who texts a specific keyword to you. Not only will this help you capture your audience's contact information, but it also allows you to avoid having to pay for a guest list that often comes with presenting on stage. Plus, you can create different keywords for different events so you know where your audience is coming from and even set expiration dates to create a sense of urgency. It's a win-win situation!

> **PRO TIP:** You can get super strategic with your keyword opt-in system by creating different keywords for different events and promotions. This way, you can track where your subscribers are coming from and which campaigns are most effective. And don't forget the power of expiration! Set an expiration date for your keywords to create a sense of urgency and encourage people to take action right away instead of procrastinating. This simple trick can make a huge difference in your conversion rates.

Go On A Virtual Book Tour

Long gone are the days when you have to travel across the country sitting in bookshops to get people to notice your book. You can now jump on podcasts and guest on shows and do what I like to call "Podcast Hijacking". Let me explain.

Podcasts are an amazing way to reach a large and engaged audience, and if you're lucky enough to be a guest on a show, you have the opportunity to tap into the host's hard-earned trust and build a relationship with their listeners. These shows can be around for life, and people are often searching podcasts for solutions to specific problems, so if you're able to share your story and process on a show, you can potentially attract new clients for years to come. Plus, the best part is that podcast listeners are already audio lovers, so you don't have to convince them to give your audiobook a chance. All you have to do is share your keyword opt-in and you can easily capture all those listeners for your own audience.

There are several ways to get on people's podcasts as a guest, and it all starts with building relationships with potential hosts. One way to do this is to reach out to hosts directly and pitch yourself as a guest sharing how your appearance will help the host's audience.

Another way to get on podcasts is to shout your expertise to high Heavens on social media, making yourself known to potential hosts. Get loud on your own blog or social media channels, and promote any appearances you make on other podcasts or in the media. This can help you build your reputation and increase your visibility, which can lead to more opportunities to be a guest on other podcasts.

Finally, consider joining masterminds or groups because they're swimming with podcast hosts. By getting loud, sharing your accomplishments and making relationships, you start to get a flood of invites to people's shows.

While you're at it, offer to teach your solution to their communities. Ask to be a guest speaker or teacher to their group, whether it's a coaching group, Facebook group, or bingo group. It doesn't matter. Getting in front of other people's audiences is great way to hijack them.

Later on in this guide I'm sharing the fast track to audio profits. In fact, the opportunities are endless. These are just some easy quick wins that you can do immediately.

The $5 Ad Strategy

When you join our program, we go deeper into more ways to profit but I want to give you just one more incredible strategy using cheap $5 ads. To be clear, talking about online ads can be an entire chapter (or book) and this is just a quick tip to get you started.

Social media sites like Facebook and Instagram offer an ad type called "form ad". The view taps a button and a short form appears that is already filled in with their details. So the viewer taps again and don't even leave Facebook. These ads are cheaper to run because most don't know how to use them. But I'm going to share how you can use them and grow your list like wild fire.

You set up an ad that promotes your audiobook. You have an image of your book and short text about how it will help them (ask AI to write you some ad copy). Then connect that form to your Hiro account so they automatically get your audiobook when they fill out the form. Now they didn't even have to leave Facebook and they got your book and you got their details.

We normally run these ads with a maximum spend of only $5 a day and it works like gangbusters. And as a special note, after the view sends you their details, you can direct them to a testimonial page to really hammer home the great decision they just made.

THE $5 LIST BUILDER

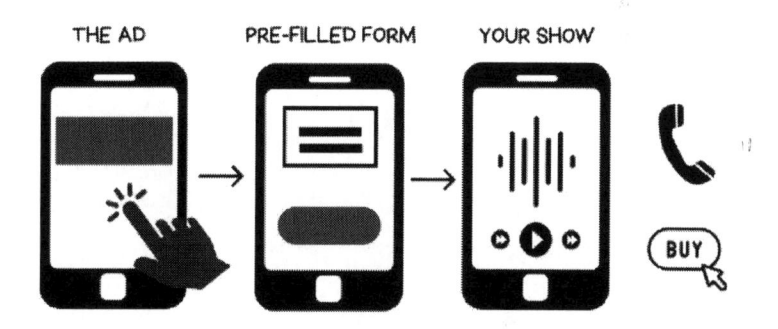

THE AD → **PRE-FILLED FORM** → **YOUR SHOW** → BUY

HOMEWORK:

1. Create you simple 2-3 sentence "Hand Raiser" post on social media
2. Share your post in the Super Hiro Facebook group

Key Takeaways:

- To make a call with you seem like a gift from the gods, let the reader know exactly what will happen when they take action

- Turn "no's" into "not yet" by giving the reader instructions on what they can do to position themselves to work with you.

- Use the 'hand raiser' post to test your book ideas, get your first customers and kill procrastination.

- Go on a virtual book and teaching tour to "hijack" other people's audiences for your own list.

- Use our $5 ad process to grow a huge list to promote your new book to and get to the Amazon best seller list.

UP Next:

> In the next section, I'm going to show you how to create a private podcast that connects with your audience on a deeper level and makes them want to hire you without even having to create a new audiobook or pick up a microphone. Yes, you're in luck, because in the next section, I'm going to show you exactly how to do that. This system is seriously powerful and can be used in your show, as well as any speaking or teaching events you participate in. And the best part? You don't even have to write anything. So buckle up and get ready to learn how to create a podcast that speaks directly to your audience's frustrations, hopes, and innermost secrets.

CHAPTER 7: The Fastest Path to Audio Cash

Before you sit down and push out an entire audiobook, I want to ask you a question. Do you have any courses that are only half-finished, or maybe some Q&As that aren't making any money? Or maybe you have a course that you launched, but your students can't find the time to complete it, like our friend Kiana. If you answered yes to any of these questions, then you're in luck.

Your quickest path to profits is to use resources you already have and create an audio version. Many of our customers start by reusing existing materials at first. They create new audiobook later on. It's easier than you think - with just some Q&A's and an unfinished course on the hard drive. I'm about to show you how easy it can be cash-in quickly.

Are up ready to transform those dusty files into money?

Do you have audios or videos from...

- Online courses
- Coaching calls
- Q&A's
- Summits
- Challenges
- Live events

Check places like Google Drive, Dropbox and backup drives. You never know what you'll find!

If you have any existing courses or materials that are collecting dust on your hard drive, you can easily turn them into profitable audio products. All you have to do is create an audio version and offer it to your existing customers at a reduced price. Even if they don't buy it, you can still make money by offering it as an extra product to your program. I wouldn't give it away for free, though. Here's why:

Studies show that only 3% of all courses are completed because most students to struggle to find the time to go through all the material. And sometimes, students will ask for a refund because they don't have the time to complete the course. But instead of giving them a refund, you can offer them the audio version for free. This small gesture can go a long way in retaining those students and boosting your profits. So don't be afraid to sell the audio versions of your existing materials - it can be a great way to increase your profits and help more people.

If you give something away for free, people will often treat it like it's not worth anything. But if you charge for it upfront and then offer it as a gift later on, it sends a much stronger message. This is because people value things that they have to pay for more than things that are given to them for free. So even if you plan to offer something for free eventually, it's best to charge for it upfront and then give it away as a bonus. This will help your audience see the value in what you're offering and take action.

EVERYTHING YOU NEED TO CREATE A HIGH CONVERTING AUDIOBOOK

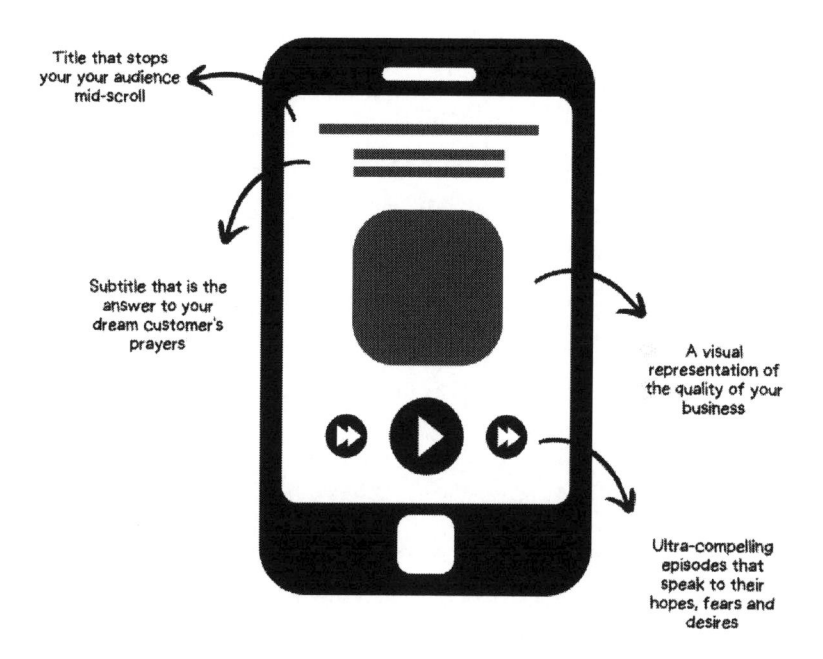

Title that stops your your audience mid-scroll

Subtitle that is the answer to your dream customer's prayers

A visual representation of the quality of your business

Ultra-compelling episodes that speak to their hopes, fears and desires

Image 9-1

Ways To Profit From Existing Content

Just like with your audiobook, you can make turn your audio products into list builders, order bumps or stand alone products. Here's how:

1. Order Bump - This is an additional product that they buyer can tack on to their main purchase. This is how you can make more money with a course.

2. One time offer - This is a product that the buyer can only get after purchasing the main product. For example,

101

when you get this coaching program, I'll give you the chance to get my audio product for half price right now, but never again anywhere else.

3. Special offer - This is great for when you launch your audiobook or products for the first time. You can offer them for a reduced rate to a select number of people for a limited time. Then the price goes up.

4. Out of the vault - This works wonderfully if you want to reuse an event or coaching program from the past that you no longer sell. My friend, Myron Golden, did this with coaching calls he hosted back in the day when we all had to dial in on a regular phone because online calls didn't exist and it sold like gangbusters.

> **PRO TIP:** Do you have a YouTube channel? With Hiro, you can import your entire channel and instantly create a private podcast from your channel. You can offer the private podcast to your subscribers and viewers and build your email list.

Case Studies

Gina Mooran used Hiro to turn her weekly Q&A calls into a private podcast for her students. She sent an email to her list of 7,000 subscribers, offering access to the podcast for half off ($7) with a 3-day expiration. After the launch, she raised the price to $14 per month.

In addition to the email, Gina also went live in her Facebook group to share the benefits of listening to her Q&A show. As a result of these efforts, she made over $3,000 on her launch.

This is a great example of how using Hiro create fast profits and help your audience in a more engaging way.

Another example is my friend Chimine who used Hiro to turn a live, in-person event from two years ago into a private podcast. She emailed her list, offering access to her show for $67.

Like Gina, Chimine made a few grand as well. The funny thing is that her sales page was broken. She had white text on a white background. People were entering their credit card and couldn't even see if their digits were correct. It was a disaster. She lost out on so many sales, because we didn't discover it until days later.

The point is, people want to have these audio products. There is demand for it, and they'll even use "invisible order forms" to get it. So don't feel like you have to record something new.

> **PRO TIP**: How to double your sales
>
> Did you know that McDonald's makes over $10 million a day from the Happy Meal? That's right - the inclusion of a small toy in the meal boosts their sales by 40%. This just goes to show that people are willing to pay extra for something they perceive as valuable, even if it's just a small added bonus. So if you're looking to increase your sales, consider offering a bonus to your audio show.
>
> In other words, if you have a course, sprinkle in a Q&A session from your premium clients, some interviews that aren't available anywhere else, or trainings from your mentors.
>
> Suddenly your show isn't just a copy of the original product. Whether it's an ebook, and you have an audio version, or a course and you have an audio version, or a summit and you

> have an audio version, put something else in the audio version that wasn't available in the original product to make it even better.

How To Create A Show Without Picking Up A Mic

Let's say you don't have any prior created content. You don't have any courses, or interviews, or anything in your Zoom folder. And you don't want to use AI to create an audiobook. You flat out don't want to record anything either.

I got your back. There are private label rights, content already pre-made around thousands of subjects that you can purchase the rights to. Meaning, you can legally use that content as your own and profit from it.

Google "PLR" and you will find a bunch of websites with content that you can purchase the rights for ten or twenty bucks. You can then turn that content into your own private podcast.

> **PRO TIP:** Your content doesn't have to be in audio format because you can upload the videos to Hiro and Hiro will convert them into audio.

You can then create your show using pre-made content. You don't even have to pick up a microphone to start building your list, book more calls and sell more products.

Key Takeaways:

- You don't have to create an audiobook to start profiting from audio. You can use content you already have like courses, Q&A's, interviews, and events

- Make your audio product even more irresistible by adding in something that your book doesn't have, like in depth interviews. This works for courses and other audio products as well.

- Don't give away the audio version of your course as part of your course bundle. Instead, sell it so you can later offer it as a gift for anyone struggling to find time to watch the videos.

Homework:

1. Take any videos or audios from past events and put them in a folder titled "Hiro"

2. Log into Hiro and turn your content into an audio product

3. Sell access to this audio product or give it away for free to build your list

Up Next

Once you have your show set up, the next step is to gain some free marketing. Do you want thousands of people to hear about your audiobook for free? Keep reading to learn how to get more listeners for your show.

CHAPTER 8: How to Get Free Exposure to Thousands of Listeners

Want to get thousands of new listeners for your show? Here's what to do:

1. Create your audiobook or private podcast in Hiro and make it "live".
2. Create mock ups of your show using Canva.com
3. Post the mockups on social media and tag us (@heycarlawhite and @heyhirofm)

We will share your show to our audience and your get free listeners. Plus, you will get a chance to be featured on our podcast too.

Remember, we can only share your show if you let us know it's out there, so make sure to tag us and post it on social media!

In the next section, I'll show you how to quickly grow your audience and keep them engaged with a powerful combination of audiobooks, memberships, courses, and more. Plus, I'll reveal how you can get six months of access to Hiro for free.

Would you love to have Hiro for free?

I will share a special bonus that is only available to people who get this guide. If you want to continue profiting from cutting-edge technology that's available nowhere else, then keep reading. I'm gonna pull back the curtain and share everything!

CHAPTER 9: What's next?

We've covered a lot so far, haven't we? Let's reset. Let's breathe for a second. Because it's a lot to digest, right? We've covered a summary of 14 years of perfecting methods, millions of dollars worth of sales for me and for 1,000's of my clients.

We covered it in a very short amount of time together. I condensed, squeezed it all together as tightly as possible and created a whole step-by-step process for hyper-automation. But here's the reality.

Even if you just used a tiny fraction of what we covered today, don't you feel like you've taken a giant leap forward with your business? Yes!

I don't know what you knew about interactive audiobooks, AI, and automations when you started reading this guide, but is it safe to say that some of what we covered was new and invaluable to you? Yes!

Stuff like my Automated Sales Machine that you can plug into your business to create more buyers and position yourself as the authority than most people. And my Perfect Book Formula that you'll be able to use in other areas of your business, not just for your books and audiobooks.

You can use my Done In A Day with tools and technology take an idea to market in less time, with less tech, less team, while giving yourself a competitive edge that stands out from the competition.

Or, apply my Hand Raiser Post Method that kills your procrastination and perfectionism, while creating a rush of buyers without even spending a dime!

Or my Simple Three Text System, that you can easily drop into any audio show, for bringing them back to the show, getting them to your calls, or getting probably more money than any of us deserve.

And, you can do it in one sitting in a single afternoon. All that and much, much more.

This leads to my next question for you. Do you feel that our time together thus far has been well spent? Yes!

And now, do you feel more confident and compelled with using AI, audio, automations, and new technologies in your business? Yes!

And can you see how even a little bit, just the one or two things I showed you today, can help your business regardless of whether you use it in audios or elsewhere? Yes!

And are you excited to make a go of it and see what wonderful things will open up in your life? Yes!

That's great because I sincerely hope that you enjoyed this guide. I tried my best to offer you a proven process for leveraging technologies of the future in your business incredibly fast.

However, what will make Automated Selling Machine incredibly successful in your business isn't just one audiobook. But a strategic combination of audio products that brings in a flood of leads, turns them from **cold to sold**, and delivers your expertise. This is mastery.

At this point, you have two options. Option one, you can read this guide a hundred times to and work on your book alone every day throughout hundreds of attempts to get better and better.

Or option two, you can shortcut the entire process and have me and my team do it with you.

Imagine getting your hands on all **the shortcuts, tools and exact steps** to launching your audiobook and physical book using my entire team as well as all my secrets? We're talking all the nuts and bolts so it's Sesame Street Simple.

What if our team takes care of all the scary tech too so that you can get your books online with more confidence and less confusion?

Would it help to see my **exact process** to attracting listeners, getting them to hit play and binge your awesome book? Then your readers doing your marketing for you by sharing it with family and friends.

You'll also learn exciting new ways for you to monetize. Things I wish I knew when I first got into audio.

Plus you we give you six months of Hiro premium absolutely free!

Introducing the Prompt Publish Profit Sprint

I've taken everything I've learned from helping thousands of entrepreneurs just like you profit from publishing and turned it into a 5-Step Process to launch your book in less than a month (many do it way faster than that).

We give you the entire system, from prompt to publish to making you an authority in your field.

I'm handing over the step-by-step process to get there.

While everyone else is tire kickers and time wasters, you'll be closing deals for breakfast.

A Sneak Peak Inside The Sprint

Step-by-step on creating your automated selling system. I wanted to devote an entire masterclass on what it looks like to use one book to grow your list, nurture and bring in revenue over and over again.

I give you my "fill-in-the-blank" instant audiobook formula and walk you through have AI write everything for you.

I also give you my behind-the-scenes process that $1B companies like Clubhouse use to quickly grow and how you can use the exact system with your audiobook.

We not only make you far, far more money faster than if you did it all yourself, we also take the massive burden of figuring it all out and profiting from audio off your shoulders.

To quantify that in real terms, 100% of our Masterclass members cover their investment instantly by making one or two additional sales the first month.

And if you don't believe you can make a couple extra sales by adding hyperautomated machine to your business then we show you how to offer this service to others. You become a audiobook expert and help others profit.

> **PRO TIP:** Get someone else to invest in the masterclass for you by offering to set up their shows for free in exchange for covering the course cost. This gets your the training and your first customer.

But if you're determined to use this process and do it yourself, we encourage you to do that. Actually, that's one of the reasons why I created this guide. If you use this and it increases your sales, we ask that you share this guide or the audiobook with your peers.

We appreciate you becoming a valuable member of the Super Hiro community simply by spreading the word about Hiro.

Additionally, if you're looking for more resources like you've experienced in our quick guide, then head over to Hiro.fm. Look trainings from me, my mentors, and other Super Hiros like you.

Finally, please remember before we leave that the biggest expense in your business is lost attention, which costs you lost sales. If you're tired of fighting for attention, and missing sales, use audio religiously and Prompt Publish Profit method with Hiro.fm!

About the Author

Founder and CEO of Hiro.fm, Carla White, is a trailblazing software pioneer, best selling author, podcast host, and coach who helps entrepreneurs profit using software of the future. She was the first woman to launch an iPhone app, and has been featured in numerous publications, including Oprah, NBC, and the NY Times.

After getting an MBA, working at the Pentagon and learning how to speak multiple languages, Carla found herself living out of her car and eating leftovers off of people's plates. She went from having $47 in her pocket to flying first class around the world by profiting from powerful, new-era technology.

Carla is committed to sharing her systems with others while offering software, coaching and premium white glove services for entrepreneurs to make a bigger impact.

She is the mother of two adorable boys and one naughty puppy. She also sits on the boards of various nonprofits that support adoption, mental health and women in leadership.

Next Steps:

Whenever you're ready, here are 4 ways we can help you grow you business:

1. Have us build your Automated Selling Machine

If you are interested in having us create your Automated Selling Machine that catapults your authority and sales, we can build it for you. All you have to do is show up for a couple of interviews and our team does the rest. Email hello@hiro.fm with "Build It" in the subject line.

2. Learn all my secrets on Prompt - Publish - Profit

If you are an entrepreneur who wants to get your hands on all **the shortcuts, tools and exact steps** to launching not just one profitable private podcast, but a library of them? We're talking all the nuts and bolts so the path to profits is Sesame Street simple. Plus Hiro for completely free, then go to **promptpublishprofit.com/join** right now

3. Have Carla speak at your event

If you are invested in having myself, Carla White, speak at your event, send and email to hello@hiro.fm with "Speaking" in the subject line.

4. Need something else?

Send an email to hello@hiro.fm and let us know how we can help!

What Others Are Saying About Hiro.fm

This is the fastest way to create my courses You can turn content into moola! It's so good! I have two kids, a business and ADHD and can create a new product in a day with this!

– Nellie Corriveau, CEO

Carla is one of the smartest people I've met when it comes to business, marketing and discovering trends that work now. When she talks, I take notes.

– Eileen Wilder, Million Dollar Speaker

Now I can reach a higher level of clients. People who refuse to get on Zoom or watch videos because they are running million dollar businesses.

– Wie Houng, Inventor and CEO

Everyone should use audio in their business and Carla has one of the best softwares around.

– Russell Brunson, Founder of ClickFunnels

Resources & Checklists

Software and Materials Needed:

Hiro - to produce you audiobook (https://hiro.fm)
ChatGTP - to help write your book (https://openai.com)
Canva - for marketing materials (https://canva.com)
Fiverr - to format your book and create cover art (https://fiverr.com)
Amazon KDP account - to publish your physical book (https://kdp.amazon.com)

CREATE PROFILE CHECKLIST

Prepare:

- Get a profile picture (this will be shown in the app) Get your logo (sqare is best)
- Have a Stripe account
- Get your Hiro affiliate account (Sign up at https://hiro.fm/partner)
- In Hiro, click on the square with your initial in the upper right corner of the screen

Setup Profile:

- Click on Profile Page Settings
- Upload your photo and logo - SAVE CHANGES

- Update your social media links - SAVE CHANGES
- Update your bio (with give you samples to make it fast) - SAVE CHANGES

Test & Promote:

- Scroll to the top and click "View Profile Page" and see if you like everything
- Copy profile page link and add it to your bios, email signatures and web pages

If your listeners join Hiro, we pay you:

- Click on "Partnership" tab in your profile settings
- Add your affiliate id so you make money from anyone who joins Hiro from your shows

Connect Stripe:

- Click on "Integrations" (bottom of the left sidebar) Click connect button and follow the steps

CREATE SHOW CHECKLIST

Steps to setting up your show in Hiro

Prepare:

- Get Hiro account & login
- Put audios / videos in a "Hiro" folder
- Create doc with episode titles and descriptions
- Create your show cover art (Canva is great)

Create:

- In Hiro, hover over "Shows", click the + and "New Show" Select "Start from scratch"
- Enter your show details & cover art Set feed release & expiration
- Bulk upload audios / videos
- Click on each episode to update the title and description (copy and paste from your doc)
- Make show and episodes "LIVE"

Test:

- Add yourself as a listener
- Click Listeners, click + and "single listener"
- Add your name, phone number and email
- Install show on the Hiro app and play it
- Take a screenshot of your show and send it to your computer for mockups
- Congrats! You set up your show!

SETUP SALES PAGE

Steps to setting up your no-code sales page

Prepare:

- Testimonial copy and images
- Two paragraphs about your show (we give you examples on your sales page settings)
- FAQ's

Setup:

- In Hiro, click on your show title in the side bar. This opens the show settings.
- Click the "Money" tab at the top (Next to Overview and Settings)
- Update the domain URL if you want it different that what is defaulted - SAVE
- Enter some description about your show. Use the examples to help you get started - SAVE
- Add your reviews - SAVE
- Update the FAQ's - SAVE
- Scroll to top of page and click "Overview" tab

Make live, test and share:

- Make Sales Page Live - Turn on
- Click "Sales Page" button to view it
- Click Share and "Copy sales page URL" to paste the URL on your emails, webpages and social media profiles

SETUP KEYWORD

Steps to setting up your keyword optin

Setup:

- In Hiro, click on Keyword and New Keyword Set the status of published or scheduled. If scheduled, then set the go live date
- Enter your keyword. (Tip: make it easy to spell and memorable)

- Select the show or shows you want to send in the text message. You can send them access to as many shows as you like.
- Update the "Collect Email" and "Collect Name" messages if you want to
- Save Keyword

Test:

- Text the keyword to the dedicated number to test

AUTOMATIONS CHECKLIST

Steps to setting up your automations

Create:

- Click on "Automations" and "New"
- Select the show you want the automations to happen (you only select one show)
- Select your trigger event
- Select what to trigger (message, email, etc) Enter in the details and CONFIRM
- Create another automation for the same trigger or create another trigger
- Save and test your automations

AI Prompts To Get You Started

The Basics

What is a prompt?

Artificial intelligence tools like ChatGTP write content by using a process called "prompting," which is basically just giving the AI a starting point or theme to work with. So let's say you want to write a story about a group of friends who go on a wild adventure. You could give ChatGPT a prompt like "friends on an adventure" and it would generate all sorts of ideas and text for you to use as inspiration.

How to write the perfect prompt for ChatGTP?

Clearly state 1) the task or question you want the AI to help with 2) provide any necessary context or information and 3) be specific and concise to ensure the AI understands what you're asking.

Why are perfect prompts important?

Because they affect the quality of the results you get from ChatGTP.

Useful tips

1. Clearly define your goal. What do you want to achieve with your prompt? Are you looking to generate ideas, create content, or something else? Clearly defining your

goal will help you create a prompt that is focused and effective.

2. Keep it simple. The best prompts are straightforward and easy to understand. Avoid using jargon or overly complex language.

3. Make it specific. The more specific your prompt is, the more focused the responses from ChatGPT will be. So instead of asking a general question, try to be as specific as possible.

4. Use action words. Prompts that use action words like "create," "design," or "write" can help ChatGPT understand what you want it to do.

It's super easy to get amazing results with ChatGPT as long as you use the right prompts. Remember, the better your prompts, the better your results will be.

Bad Example:

"Can you give me the tea on what's going on with the royals? I'm trying to get a handle on the spare."

Good Example:

"What's the latest news on the Royal Family and Prince Harry's recent book called "The Spare"?

Hacks

Adding these to your prompts or conversations with ChatGTP will help with the results. These are constantly evolving so be sure to sign up for our Prompt-Publish- Profit Extra to get more.

Pretend you are [insert character] - this is powerful to get a response in the viewpoint of a person like a travel agent, author, plumber. For example, Pretend you are a 4th grader and explain nuclear physics.

Continue, go on, and then?, more - ChatGTP has a word limit so if you want a longer response, you need to request that it writes more. Responding with a word like "more" will then get ChatGTP to write more on the same response.

In the tone of [insert famous name] - if you want your book to be in a certain language, then you might have to train ChatGPT first by sharing some writings by that person. If that person is well know, you could just instruct ChatGPT to use that artist's tone. For example, *"Write some tips on how to get started with ChatGTP in the tone of Dr Seuss."*

Book Prompt Basics

ChatGPT can produce output is impressive but it's not perfect. Often you miss some creativity and I would say that the output is too literal. As I learn more how to talk better to AI's and ChatGPT, I discover new and better ways to write stories. So be sure to sign up for our Prompt-Publish- Profit Extra to get more at **promptpublishprofit.com/extra**

Book Title:

- Write a list of book titles based on [concept/topic] for [target audience]

Subtitle:

- Write a list of book subtitles based on [concept/topic] for [target audience]

Book Description:

- Write a summary of a book about [concept/topic] for [target audience]

Call to action:

- Write a call to action to buy this book

Introduction

Hook:

- Write a compelling personal story based on [concept/topic] for [target audience]
- Write the big outcome the reader will get from the book.
- Write a shocking fact based on [concept/topic] for [target audience]
- Write an uncommon belief based on [concept/topic] for [target audience]
- Write an amazing discovery that the reader will learn at the end.
- Write a shocking statement about why people/institutions/organizations don't want you to know about [concept/topic]

Value

- What value is this? Monetary value? Time value? Freedom value? Other values?

> **PRO TIP:** Personal stories, shocking facts, and options contradictory to popular belief are great ways to hook a reader

This Book Is For You...

- Write a paragraph about who this book is for
- Write a paragraph about who this book is not for

> **PRO TIP:** Call out internal desires and remove present pain, then expand. Example:
>
> - Are you tired of ...
> - Do you want more ...
> - Are you ready for ...
> - Have you already tried...

Skeptics Read This...

- What would a skeptical person say about this concept, topic, or idea
- If you are concerned X - the answer is Y (repeat for all objections the reader may have)

> **PRO TIP:** This is for objection handling. Call it out here and address the concept, topic, or idea you want to relate to the skeptics

- This book is still for you even if X, Y, Z

How This Book Is Different

- What are 3 ways this book is different?

How To Read This Book

- How should someone read this book based on the concept, topic, or idea?
- How should the reader commit to the actions outlined in this book?

> **PRO TIP:** help your audience with overwhelm and Give them direction

Open Loop

- What captivating hook for what is coming next in the book?

Your Story

This is your backstory but it's also your listener's story if they follow your process. The entire point of this section is for people to feel like they actually know you when you're done. The more vulnerable you are, the more impact your story is going to have on the people reading or listening to your book. Impact is what keeps people hooked so we want to make as much impact as possible.

I usually follow a simple outline:

- Tell a quick story about your childhood and upbringing. Who are you? Who were your parents and siblings?
- Tell them HOW and WHY you started doing what you are doing now.
- Explain how your success has impacted your family and those around you. What good have you done in the world because of the success you've had?

- Share any awards or accolades you've been given for being an expert in your field.
- Sell the reader on the opportunity by sharing my "before and after" story. Give yourself a "before" identity and an "after" identity.
- Why should they believe in me, belief in themselves, have full confidence and clarity they are on the right path
- Build authority by sharing your results, positioning, celebrity connections, testimonials
- Conclude by building hope for a future that is much better than the present
- Get the reader to commit to taking action so that they can have that better future
- Get the reader to commit to the new identity.

> **PRO TIP:** Sell them on 3 things:
> - Right opportunity? (book)
> - Right person? (author)
> - Right time? (them)
> - New identity (old you vs new you)
> "If not this, then what? If not you, then who? If not now, then when?"

Creating Your Outline:

Use this section for brainstorming, then come back, organize, and insert in a logical order based on the flow of the book.

Outline:

- write a book outline about [concept/topic] for [target audience]

Chapter 1: Problem you are solving.

Ask yourself: Why is it important to solve this problem?

- Write a problem we are solving based on the concept, topic, or idea you want to relate to the readers
- Write an introductory paragraph about the biggest problem relating to the concept, topic, or idea you want to relate to the readers
- Write a chapter outline based on the concept, topic, or idea above
- Write a chapter conclusion paragraph with action steps based on the concept, topic, or idea above

Chapter 2: History of the problem

Ask yourself: Where did it all start? Where are we now?

- What's the history of the problem we are solving based on the concept, topic, or idea you want to relate to the readers
- Write an introductory paragraph about the problem history relating to the concept, topic, or idea you want to relate to the readers
- Write a chapter outline based on the concept, topic, or idea above
- Write a chapter conclusion with action steps based on the concept, topic, or idea above

Chapter 3: Introduce Your Unique Method for Creating this Change

Ask yourself: Why is your method different?

- Write about the unique method for solving the problem based on the concept, topic, or idea in the content brief

- Write a chapter outline based on the concept, topic, or idea above
- Write about the pain without your method for creating this change
- Describe the future with this method. Get them to take action in their mind using a story.
- Share a story about the future outcome
- Write a chapter conclusion paragraph with action steps based on the concept, topic, or idea above

Chapters 4-9: Your Steps For Creating Change

What do we need to do first?

Second?

Third?

- Write a story based on the concept, topic, or idea you want to relate to the readers
- Introduce the topic of this chapter
- Write a chapter outline based on the topic of this chapter
- Write why this is important
- Write about the "hell" without this step
- Write about the "heaven" with this step
- Write about the "how to"
- Sell them on the possibilities of implementing this step
- Write action steps to get a quick win from this step
- Write a chapter conclusion paragraph with action steps based on the concept, topic, or idea above

> **PRO TIP:** Rinse and repeat for each chapter, modify the commands based on the concept, topic, or idea based on the content brief

Chapter 10: What the Future Holds

- What is coming in the future for based on the concept, topic, or idea in the content brief
- Write a story based on the concept, topic, or idea you want to relate to the readers
- Introduce the topic of this chapter
- Write a chapter outline based on the topic of this chapter
- Write a chapter conclusion paragraph with action steps based on the concept, topic, or idea above

Conclusion

5-7 answers you covered in the book

- Summarize the concepts covered in each chapter based on the content brief
- Write six "yes" questions

Next Steps:

- Thank the reader
- Write a call to action for the next steps

Research, Resources and Appendix

- List all the tools needed for the journey.

Printed in Great Britain
by Amazon